In Our Time

Paul H. Douglas

IN OUR TIME

 Harcourt, Brace & World, Inc.   New York

To all those who in crowded precincts and in all the walks of life have been my comrades and my inspiration as we worked together for justice, peace and freedom during these last tumultuous forty years

Preface

This book is the outgrowth of a series of lectures which I gave at the New School for Social Research in New York City during the winter of 1967. I have tried to amplify the subject matter of these lectures and bring them up to date. The first of them has already appeared in *The American Scholar* for Winter 1967–68 and is reprinted here with the permission of the editors.

I am indebted to many persons who have helped in the collection and interpretation of the material, among whom I should like to mention and thank Howard Shuman, Mollie Orshansky, Thomas Vail, Kenneth McLean and Kenneth Gray. I am especially indebted to my very efficient and cheerfully patient secretary, Mrs. Jane Enger, and her associates, for the continuous process of typing and retyping illegible manuscripts so that the book itself might appear. I am also indebted to Katherine Douglas for helping with the proofs and preparing the index and to Ellen Kelly, who assisted me with the tables.

The issues which are discussed are some of those in which I have been personally involved and with which I believe the American public should become increasingly concerned in our time.

—PAUL H. DOUGLAS

Washington, D.C.
June 17, 1968

Contents

Preface   v

1   The Problem of Tax Loopholes
     (Or: My Eighteen Years in a Quandary and
     How It Grew)   1

2   The Oil Shale Treasure and Attempts to Despoil It   29

3   Some Ethical Problems of Politicians   70

4   Truth in Lending   94

5   The Extent and Contours of Poverty   123

6   The Reduction in Poverty   144

7   Public Efforts to Reduce Poverty   154

8   Cash Supplements and Work for the Poor   194

     Index   223

1

The Problem of Tax Loopholes (Or: My Eighteen Years in a Quandary and How It Grew)

By the summer of 1950, the attack by the North Koreans upon South Korea had plunged us into a full-scale Asiatic war. North Korea was being egged on and equipped by Red China and Russia, and the war was another effort by the Communist bloc to take over additional territory.

President Truman and the United Nations rose to the occasion and resisted this aggression, and it became necessary to raise large additional sums of money, running into many billions of dollars.

As the new tax bills moved onto the floor of the Senate, Senator Hubert Humphrey and I became more aware of the injustices in the existing tax structure and of the new abuses that were being added.

Although we were only freshmen, and were not members of
the Finance Committee, we felt it our duty both to become
better educated on tax matters and to work for a more just
revenue system. We believed this was particularly necessary
because thousands of young Americans were being killed and
many more were being wounded, and we felt that here at
home profiteering should be reduced to a minimum.

A tax seminar was therefore organized which was attended
by some members of the liberal bloc of Senators. We got public-spirited experts to coach us in these secret sessions and to
conduct what was, in effect, a cram course. Then, with fast-
beating hearts, we ventured out on the floor to do battle
with the two shrewdest minds of the Senate—Walter George
and Eugene Millikin, both of whom had impressive reputa-
tions and an awe-inspiring capacity for thunderous debate.
We also had to face, on some issues, Tom Connally of Texas,
who loved to lash his opponents with the bullwhip of his
brutal sarcasm, and who treated dissenters as though they
were pre–Civil War slaves in the cotton kingdom or ram-
bunctious horses to be subdued by lash and spur. Tom had
traces of frontier populism, but he also had a deep hatred of
Northern liberal Democrats, which made us fair game.

For many days we fought on a variety of issues. It seemed
an unequal struggle, since George, Millikin and Connally not
only had the votes, but also had many years' acquaintance
with the intricacies of the tax code, and were equipped with
a formidable bevy of tax experts at their elbows, while we had
to stand alone.

We had to learn and learn fast, and to deal on our feet with
a baffling series of arguments which in retrospect prove to
have been sophistical, although at the time they were persuasive. The press galleries were unsympathetic and our fellow Senators largely hostile.

We had a rough time, but the longer the discussion went on

the more convinced I became that the tax code was, in fact, permeated with favors to particular groups and individuals, and that it violated what seemed to be an elemental principle of equity, namely, that people with approximately equal net incomes should pay approximately equal taxes. Despite all the battering we received, and the loss of prestige we suffered, both Senator Humphrey and I felt that the correctness of our positions had been maintained under fire.

So apparently did some of the experts, because there shortly appeared able articles by two eminent lawyers—William L. Carey, of Northwestern and Columbia, and Stanley Surrey, then of Harvard University—that echoed our criticisms. The dean of tax lawyers, the late Randolph Paul, in public testimony also stressed many of the points we had tried to advance.

In 1955, I became chairman of the Joint Economic Committee, and with the able staff assistance of Dr. Norman Ture, the committee began to assemble evidence and take skilled testimony on many of the inequities that we had spotted. In the same year, after a long struggle, and largely because of the persistence of columnist Doris Fleeson, I was finally placed on the Senate Finance Committee, where I served for the next eleven years until my defeat for a fourth term in 1966.

On the Finance Committee I saw the formation of tax policy at first hand and took part in the intimate discussions that attended the writing and revision of our tax laws. I continued to urge most of the reforms that Senator Humphrey and I had advocated in 1950 and 1951 and, in addition, discovered new abuses that I thought needed to be corrected. After a little while, I was joined by Senator Albert Gore of Tennessee, who proved to be a strong and public-spirited colleague.

It was a tough decade. On major issues where enormous

sums were at stake, we were almost always defeated, whether in committee or on the floor. But in the process we gained minor changes that reduced some of the specific injustices, so that we were never completely discouraged or frustrated.

There were two general sets of facts that convinced me that there were great abuses within our federal tax system.

The first was that only about half of the total personal income in the country was subject to taxation, while the other half completely escaped. The basic exemption of $600 a person accounted for only a fraction of this latter amount. The remainder was largely income that most people believed was taxable but which in reality was exempted by a series of devices.

Then we discovered, and got the Treasury to confirm, that in every year there were a considerable number of persons with annual incomes of over $500,000 who paid no taxes at all. As we gathered evidence we found this number would never fall below twenty-five and sometimes went above thirty.* We also found an even greater number with huge incomes who paid less than 10 or 15 percent.

We found that the averages paid by the groups with incomes above $50,000 was only a fraction of the amount they were presumed to pay, and that the uppermost group with incomes over $250,000, who according to the schedules were presumed to pay nearly 90 percent, actually paid on the average only 25 percent or slightly less. The "effective" rate was therefore far less than the nominal rate.

All this, plus the evidence on specific "loopholes" or "truckholes" that enabled large quantities of income to slip through the tax net, still further convinced Senator Gore and me that we should expose these abuses and seek to cure them. We continued to be helped by public-spirited experts, who gave

* The *Statistics of Income* for 1965, p. 8, shows 35 individuals with incomes over $500,000 who paid no taxes (i.e., column 1 minus column 5). If we were to count all capital gains as income, this number would probably be trebled.

us surreptitious information, sometimes at real risk to themselves, and in particular by the ability of my former assistant, Philip Stern, who, building on some of our work and adding much of his own, produced his brilliant and witty book, *The Great Treasury Raid* (New York, 1964), which is still the classic in this field.

Out of this experience of nearly two decades I have distilled certain facts and conclusions. They show that our tax system is riddled with injustices that violate the simple principle, upon which I would think that all could agree, that people with equal net incomes should pay equal or approximately equal taxes. Whether we believe in progressive, regressive or proportional taxation, can we not all agree on this elementary principle of horizontal justice?

But this experience of nearly two decades and our relative lack of success also plunged me ever more deeply into a quandary.

When the so-called Ruml plan for withholding a basic percentage of the federal income tax from wages and salaries was adopted by Congress, it did not apply the withholding principle to interest and dividends. Such income was, on the contrary, to be reported by the recipient and the taxes were to be paid by him.

The Economic Committee hearings that I held in 1955 showed that although virtually all of the wages and salaries were reported, a large volume of interest and an appreciable portion of dividends were not. It became possible to estimate the size of this gap from the reports published by the Securities and Exchange Commission and by the Treasury. Our liberal group in the Senate, therefore, began to advocate applying the withholding principle, or what the British term "payment at the source" to dividends and interest so that ownership would not receive any more favored treatment than employment.

In 1962, under President Kennedy and Secretary Dillon, the Administration adopted this provision, and the Office of Tax Analysis under Donald Lubig was most helpful in the preparation of evidence and in working out simple plans for collection. It was clear that in 1959 about a billion dollars in dividends and three billion dollars in interest were not reported, with a consequent annual loss in taxes of between $900 million and $1 billion. These unreported sums amounted to 8 percent of all dividends and 34 percent of all interest. The proportion of wages and salaries not reported in 1959 came, on the other hand, to only 3 percent. This showed the greater efficiency of the withholding method.

The Administration tax bill for 1962, therefore, contained a provision for the automatic deduction and transmission to the Treasury of 20 percent from the total sums credited to dividends and interest without specifying the individuals or their amounts, and then for the filing of claims for any excess to be made periodically by the recipients. The plan was simple and just, and was adopted by the House Ways and Means Committee and by the House itself. Senator Gore and I prepared to support it in the Senate Finance Committee and, if necessary, on the floor of the Senate itself.

We had heard rumblings of opposition, but I must admit we were not prepared for the storm that followed. Suddenly, from all over the country, but especially from Illinois, thousands of protests poured into my office. By the end of a month, I had received over sixty-five thousand such letters and other Senators had received about as many. Inquiry proved that these had been stimulated by the building and loan associations, whose main national body had launched the campaign from Chicago. The banks also helped in the letter-writing blitz.

These letters showed an extraordinary misconception of the tax. A large proportion hotly attacked the requirement for withholding as the imposition of a completely new and additional tax. They apparently thought that interest either was not income or was so sacred that it should not be taxed. This very fact was in itself eloquent proof of the widespread evasion or avoidance of the tax. It was in vain that in my initial answer I pointed out to these protesters that this was not a new tax but merely a better means of collecting an existing tax that had been widely evaded and avoided, and that their confusion was indeed ample proof of an existing general failure to report.

Another widely prevalent misconception was that the tax was a levy amounting to a 20 percent annual assessment on the total capital that a person owned. It was consequently attacked as part of a Communist scheme to confiscate all capital. It was, of course, a tax on income, not on capital. Thus on $1,000 of holdings that paid 4 per cent, the 20 percent tax would be levied on the $40 of interest and not on the principal of $1,000.

I then prepared a brief article summarizing the way in which the income tax had been avoided and evaded, and how simple the proposal was—namely, to withhold one-fifth of all payments of dividends and interest and send the totals to the Treasury. In the event of overwithholding, the individuals would then be able to file quarterly requests for refunds. I pointed out to all my correspondents that the basic income tax on wages and salaries had been similarly withheld for twenty years with only annual refunds and asked why interest and dividends should be given such especially favored treatment.

It was all in vain. No one was convinced. The tide of angry letters continued to pour in. Virtually every Senator received thousands, and many counted their letters in the tens of thousands.

The result was inevitable. By a vote of eleven to five, the withholding provision was stricken from the bill in the Finance Committee. Then, on the floor of the Senate, when I moved to restore the clause, I was overwhelmingly defeated and mustered only twenty votes.

Here we were deserted by the Administration, which evidently decided that the struggle was useless. During the entire battle, the academic profession of economists was all but silent, so that Senator Gore and I felt that we had been allowed to die on an economic Berlin Wall without a hand ever being raised to help.

But as sometimes happens, to deaden the impact of our argument, and perhaps to quiet the consciences of our opponents, it was provided that institutions should report to the Internal Revenue Bureau the names and addresses of all those to whom they paid dividends and interest as well as the amounts so paid to each. Then at the regional computer centers these amounts were to be combined and the total tax due from each person was to be computed and compared with that which had been paid.

This is being done. It requires far more detailed reports from the savings institutions than the simple reporting requirements of our proposal. It will collect less money because the burden of collection from the individuals is thrown back upon the Bureau of Internal Revenue. But it does lead to a somewhat more careful reporting by the recipients and, according to the Treasury, it has increased collections by about $250 million a year. Thus far we have, therefore, saved the taxpayers about a billion dollars. Perhaps in time, in order to avoid the red tape that has been heaped upon them, the savings institutions may lessen their opposition and consent to withholding at the source. If they do, at least around $750 million more will be saved each year for the American people. With larger interest and dividend payments the savings will be greater.

What then were the real reasons for this apparently illogical opposition? I think they were the following: A very large proportion of those who had savings accounts in the banks and shares in the building and loan institutions never drew out in cash the annual interest that accumulated on their accounts but allowed it to be added automatically to their principal. Many of these savers were sufficiently naïve not to realize fully that this increase in their capital holdings came from income. They seemed to think it came from spontaneous generation. The banks and the building and loan associations, of course, knew what was happening, but they also realized that a large share of the growth in their savings deposits was due to the accumulation of compound interest, and they did not want to have this increment of growth diminished by the amount of the tax. They had the use of the funds of which the federal government was deprived, and they wanted to hold on to them.

I left this battle with a sour taste in my mouth, but also with the realization that it could have been worse and that to save a minimum of $250 million a year for the public might not have been so bad an achievement in so imperfect a world.

The biggest and longest battle was, however, over the worst abuse of all, namely the 27½ percent depletion allowance on gas and oil. Billions of dollars are at stake here, and a little explanation of the present tax procedures in the oil industry is appropriate. The oil industry already had certain tax favors that I did not question. Of course, the deduction of operating costs from gross revenue is perfectly proper. Nor did I question the propriety of charging off the costs of the unsuccessful drillings or "dry holes" from the revenues

obtained from the successful drillings when these are conducted by the same enterprise. I did not raise any objection
to granting the industry the right to charge off in the first
year all the "intangible" drilling and development costs. These
so-called development costs comprise from 75 to 90 percent
of the total exploratory and drilling costs and were granted
the fastest of all rates of accelerated depreciation—a complete
write-off in the initial year. Men in the industry who were
secretly in favor of my stand (and there are a few) have
repeatedly assured me that this is an even more important
special favor than the depletion allowance itself. But this issue
was complicated since these costs could always be alleged
to be operating costs and hence deductible dollar for dollar
from the immediate income realized from the oil and gas.

So I determined to concentrate on the 27½ percent depletion allowance, which Hubert Humphrey and I had originally attacked in 1951 and 1952. This exempted from taxation 27½ percent of all gross income in the oil and gas industry up to 50 percent of net income, and it did this without
any limitation as to the length of time for which this exemption was to continue or the ratio of the tax rebate to the
original investment.

This provision had been inserted in our tax laws during
the 1920's when the corporate income tax was only 14 percent of net profits, and when the total amount of the tax
privilege thus conferred was not overwhelming, say, about
7 percent of the profits. But it continued to be retained after
the corporate tax had risen to 52 percent and when the depletion allowance could and commonly did cut in half the
taxes paid by this rich industry. Moreover, it had spawned a
series of similar exemptions: sulfur had been granted a 23
percent exemption, and a number of minerals had been allowed a 15 percent depletion grant. Coal had been allowed
10 percent. We had seen Tom Connally broaden this exemp-

tion by a 5 percent rate on clam and oyster shells, as well as on sand and gravel—although there was no danger of "dry holes" or unsuccessful explorations in these cases! Every mineral had come to be included.

We ultimately got the Treasury to tell us how much these exemptions amounted to, and their report was that in the late fifties and early sixties the total came to about $3½ billion annually with the Treasury losing about $1½ billion. Today it is undoubtedly much more.

Long before this, however, I had prepared a counterproposal which I tried out in committee and on the floor nearly every year.

This was to introduce a sliding-scale allowance that would amount to granting the existing 27½ percent on the first million dollars of annual gross income but to decrease this to 21¼ percent on gross incomes of between one and five million dollars and then to have it fall to 15 percent on all incomes over five million dollars. This would have yielded in the earlier years from $350 to $400 million a year in revenue, while in later years the gain would have been around $500 million annually. Today it would probably be still more.

I justified this differential between small and large operators on the ground that the smaller operators were not able to distribute their risks to the same degree as the big operators and companies. Their fewer drillings exposed them, therefore, to higher risks.

I must confess, however, that I also hoped that this compromise would help to split off the small operators from the huge companies and make it more possible to pass the measure. In this, I was disappointed. Although there were only two or three concerns in Illinois that had gross receipts in excess of a million dollars, nearly all of the small operators lined up behind the big companies and in bitter opposition to me. They were the dominant economic interest in one

congressional district covering the southeastern section of
the state. Most of them insisted that I was proposing to cut
their allowance to 15 percent, although this was, of course,
not the case. No explanation was effective, although finally
the more knowledgeable would privately admit that while
they understood that they would not be hurt, for the sake
of industry solidarity they must oppose the Douglas amendment and me personally. Despite all their efforts and the oil
money that poured into the state in the 1954 and 1960 election
campaigns, I had been able to beat off their attacks, and had
even carried the oil district. Their opposition continued, however, and in the Senate I had no such luck.

Despite help from Senator Albert Gore and an honorable
conservative, Senator John Williams of Delaware, we were
periodically snowed under on the Finance Committee. Indeed, I sometimes suspected that the major qualification for
most aspirants for membership on the Finance Committee was
a secret pledge or agreement to defend the depletion allowance against all attacks. I suspected, also, that campaign funds
reinforced these pledges.

Once again, we received little or no support from the Administration, which evidently thought the depletion allowance
to be "too hot to handle." And, once again, the economics
profession was largely silent, except for a few scattered
voices that correctly pointed out that the tax favors led to
overinvestment in the industry, thus causing the average return, exclusive of tax favors, on the American investment to
fall somewhat below the general average for all industry.
But the economists seemed to take little interest in tax moral-
ity. All they had eyes for was the gross national product.*

There was therefore little or no criticism from the econo-

---

* I want to exempt Joseph Pechman from this criticism. Formerly an
expert on the staff of the Treasury and now a member of the Brookings
Institution, he has been a bulwark of strength in the battle for tax reform. There may have been a few others like him.

mists of the justice of the tax advantage that helped a number of the fabulously wealthy to escape from paying any taxes whatsoever and helped many others to pay only nominal sums. There seemed to be no resentment among businesses that oil and gas companies only paid one-third to one-half the rate of taxation upon net profits paid by the main mass of American corporations. The prevailing sentiment seemed instead to be gratification that one group, at least, had been able to outwit the government and the reformers. Despite the fact that we wanted to lower the general tax rate once we had obtained greater uniformity in our tax system, and constantly stressed this point, we were about as popular among business executives as the revenue agents used to be among the mountaineers of Appalachia when they tried to put down "moonshining."

We gained a slight flicker of interest from among a few of the independents when we pointed out that the big oil companies that had concessions in Venezuela and the Persian Gulf countries were able to escape virtually all taxation by (1) successfully claiming the depletion allowance on their foreign oil (despite the fact that subsurface deposits, under Roman and national law, are the property of the state) and (2) counting as "taxes" the royalties that they paid for the extraction abroad of government-owned oil. In this way the 50 and later 75 percent payments for the extraction of the oil were not counted as an operating expense, but rather as a tax to be deducted dollar for dollar from the tax that otherwise would be paid to the United States government.

Despite all the propaganda and the pressures, there was a heroic group of Senators who stood firm. Once we got as many as thirty-eight votes, but later we slumped to twenty. Calling for a roll-call vote was in a sense like marching brave troops into the valley of political death and reducing the number of public-spirited soldiers. Therefore, toward the end

of the long bitter struggle, I would agree to a voice, rather
than a roll-call, vote in order to shield our secret supporters.
I was willing, as were my comrades Senator William Proxmire
and Senator Gore, to be marked for destruction in a cause that
we believed to be in the public interest, but we did not want
to drag down others to political disaster and re-enact the
role of Lord Raglan, who sent the noble six hundred to death
and disaster at Balaklava in the Crimean War.

Some of us have been effectively disposed of; more probably will be; but the issue remains. And as one who still
believes (perhaps foolishly) that in a democracy no issue is
settled until it is settled right, and that in the long run an
educated public opinion will prevail, I remain guardedly
hopeful. I am grateful to Senators Proxmire and Gore, as
we all should be, for keeping the issue alive, and I pray that
they may succeed where others of us have failed.

The third great abuse lies in the field of the capital gains
tax. Here the profits realized from the sale of a capital asset
that has been held for longer than six months are taxed, when
sold, at only one-half the income tax rate, but in no case at
more than 25 percent. Moreover, the amounts untaxed are
not counted as "taxable income," and hence are missing
in the statistics issued by the Treasury Department. Like the
murdered victims of the criminal syndicate, they, with the
oil and mineral depletion allowances, are given an anonymous
burial so that even their buried bodies disappear.

Philip Stern estimated in 1962 that this favored treatment
shrunk the tax base by $6 billion a year and cost the Treasury
$2.4 billion annually. But this is only the beginning. An even
greater leakage occurs when property is bequeathed. Let us
take the case of a father who buys property for $100,000 dur-
ing his lifetime, which by the time of his death is worth $1
million, or $900,000 more. His son inherits the estate and a

year later sells this same property for $1,100,000. He will pay a capital gains tax only on the $100,000 that has accrued during his ownership, while the $900,000 gain inherited from his father not only will go tax free but will be unrecorded. Stern estimates that from $12 to $13 billion thus escape taxation every year and that the Treasury annually loses an approximate added $2.9 billion.

It was such injustices in the capital gains system (and not such incidental absurdities as giving capital gains treatment to the raising of cattle but not to chickens and turkeys) that most outraged me.

To deal with the untaxed capital gains during a testator's lifetime, I proposed collection at the time of ultimate sale, but with a deduction or tax credit given for all inheritance taxes paid in the meantime on the property. In other words, if a total inheritance tax of $50,000 had been levied on this property, this would be deducted dollar for dollar from the tax ultimately realized on the capital gains.*

And if it be objected that to tax capital gains in years of bunched income would be inequitable, I constantly made it clear that I would agree to lengthen this period to any proper degree. This would reduce the total of the super-taxes that would be paid. But such conciliatory motions were overwhelmingly defeated in committee and on the floor. At first the Kennedy Administration supported the idea of taxing the inherited capital gains, but this support faded as we approached the hour of decision, while once again the voices of the economists were for the most part mute.

The treatment of stock options was, and is, an especially antisocial use of the capital gains principle.

It had been the custom of many corporations to give to a chosen group of executives the right to buy added quantities

* The fiscal purists object to even this exemption.

of stock, and for gains realized upon this to be taxed at capital gains and not at income tax rates. Very commonly this stock could be purchased at less than the market rate, thus extending the practice of the "preferred lists" that had been the common custom during the 1920's of such financial giants as the Morgan firm and Samuel Insull. If the stock fell while the option was being held, then the beneficiary was commonly freed from his option.

The plan, by creating additional claimants for the net earnings of the companies, like the preferred lists, obviously diluted the equities of the existing stockholders.

The defense given for the stock options was, of course, that they would increase the incentive of management to make profits for the companies by increasing the amount of tax-free income that they would receive. It had a side effect of concentrating executive attention upon the price of the stock rather than treating this, as I believe should be done, as merely the by-product of an efficiently managed company. It could be argued that from the companies' standpoint it would be better to make these added payments in the form of cash bonuses or a percentage of the net profits, rather than from profits from the sale of added shares of stock. But this would have meant that the added income would have been taxed at ordinary rather than at capital gains rates. In essence the stock option plan permitted executives to become wealthier than would otherwise have been possible, and to do so in a shorter period of time. It was touted as a means of helping young executives to climb the economic ladder more rapidly, although in practice the major rewards went to those in the later afternoon of their business careers. Often as members of the boards of directors they voted themselves these large tax-free bonuses.

Thanks to the valiant efforts of Senator Gore, we succeeded

in ending some of the worst abuses of the stock option plans. How much we have saved by these modifications is still unknown, but I estimate that while the gains are real they are still minor.

Another persistent loophole is the exemption from federal taxation of the interest on the bonds of state and local governments. This exemption was first enacted because of the fear that such a tax would be held unconstitutional by the courts, and also by a desire to make the financing of capital improvements easier for the state and local governments. That it has helped in the latter direction is shown by the fact that while high grade municipals are still much less safe than federal issues, their yield in March of 1967 was a full percentage point below the latter, namely, 3½ instead of 4½ percent. Without this tax advantage, the municipalities would probably have had to pay at least 4¾ percent interest and possibly 5 percent in order to float their loans. Since the total outstanding bonds issued by the state and local governments amount to approximately $100 billion, the total in interest that is saved for these bodies probably comes to somewhere around $1¼ to $1½ billion a year.

Such tax-free issues, however, become tax havens or sanctuaries for men and women in the upper income and tax brackets. Thus, when Mrs. Horace Dodge, Sr. inherited $56 million from the estate of her husband, she immediately invested all of it in state and municipal bonds and thereby removed the entire income from her fortune from federal taxation. This is a particularly attractive tax route for those in the upper income tax brackets who do not wish to play an active role in the business world. If only the existing income from these bond issues were taxed, federal receipts would be at least 50 percent on the $3½ billion that is now immune from federal taxation. This would amount to $1¾ billion.

If the federal government were to pay an outright subsidy to the local governments to compensate for these lost tax benefits, this would still net at least a half billion dollars a year for the federal government. It might indeed net more, since the interest rate, and hence the total interest payments on state and municipals, would rise. Assuming that the total interest could increase to $4½ billion, at an average tax rate of 50 percent, this could net $2¼ billion or a billion dollars more than the compensating subsidy. Unless some such action is taken, the amount of lost income will probably increase as retired men and women of wealth seek these privileged sanctuaries.

A particularly bad form of this tax subsidy to localities occurs when local and state bonds are floated to finance the construction costs of runaway factories from other parts of the country. In many Southern states this is a common practice, and it serves to draw employment away from the North and the Midwest. It creates unemployment in these sections of the country and makes it harder for the workmen up North to obtain wage increases. Both of these factors, then, depress the tax base in these areas and decrease the ability of those who hire them to pay taxes, at the very time that they create higher local relief and welfare costs.

On top of all this, the taxpayers of the North and West have to pay higher federal income taxes or else short-change the general welfare, because of this subsidy to their Southern competitors. They in effect are being asked to help finance their own economic destruction.

Thus far the massed political power of the South has been sufficiently great to prevent the closing of even this relatively tiny loophole. In self-defense, Northern and Western states are beginning to extend similar privileges, and the evil is spreading.

.   .   .

The depreciation allowances on buildings are computed on the money cost of the property to the last purchaser and not on the book value of the physical structure of the building itself. Thus if a man constructs an office building at a cost of $5 million, he can take accelerated depreciation for several years and use this as a credit against the net income from that property, or any other property that he may own. At 5 percent a year, he would thus get a credit of $250,000. If his net income from the building was $200,000, this would mean that he would pay no taxes and would have an additional credit, to be carried over, of $50,000. This could go on for at least five years, when the accelerated depreciation amounting to approximately $1.7 million would have to be greatly reduced. But office buildings enhance somewhat in value during the first years of occupancy, and it would be quite possible to sell the property for $5 million or more instead of the depreciated book value of approximately $3,300,000. The original owner would pay a capital gains tax only on the $1.7 million profit made from selling at above book value, although he had used his depreciation allowance to reduce his higher regular income tax rate.

The newcomer could, however, start taking his depreciation at 1½ times the normal rate or 3¾ percent on his $5 million purchase price instead of on the $3.3 million of book value. This, as a matter of fact, would be an important reason why he would pay the full $5 million.

After a few years a third comer might even be willing to pay $5 million, although the $3.4 million taken for depreciation might have left about $2.5 million of the original cost of $5 million.

This process could be kept up almost interminably, with the ultimate total amounts deducted for depreciation far exceeding the original cost. This practice also puts a premium upon a frequent change of ownership, which is especially injurious in the case of tenements. We would save many hundreds of millions of dollars of taxes if depreciation were to be computed upon the book value of the building rather than upon the purchase price paid, and so that the total taken could not exceed the original cost or possibly the original cost plus replacements.

The depreciation allowance is, moreover, divorced from the performance of any major replacements or repairs. It would be better if the average depreciation rate were to be lowered from $2\frac{1}{2}$ to 2 percent or less, thus assuming a life of fifty or more years, rather than forty, for the structure, and then to provide additional allowances for those major repairs and replacements to the degree that they are actually made subject to a maximum allowance in any one year or over a span of years. This would be a mighty stimulus for owners to keep houses in repair and would lessen the tendency for them to deteriorate.

There are many other quirks and loopholes in the taxation of commercial real estate that result in great losses of tax revenue, among them the "sell and lease back" arrangement. Here any gains will be taxed later only at capital gains rather than at income tax rates, while the rent payments can be deducted from gross profits as an operating cost. Time forbids going into all these complexities. But as the publications of various tax services demonstrate, they are complex and, for those who practice them, lucrative.

In 1962, the Treasury presented a mass of evidence showing excessive tax-deduction claims for travel and for entertainment. The instances presented were at once ludicrous and also, in a sense, nauseating. We were able to tighten the rules in general terms on traveling expenses although not as much as we should have done. We also restricted the deductibility of business presents to $25.00 from one person to another.

But the major expenses for entertainment have been largely legalized, and the evils of an expense-account civilization are still largely unchecked.

During our consideration of one of the major tax bills a seemingly innocent provision was inserted that later turned out to be a Trojan horse. This was to exempt from taxation all future "charitable" contributions if in eight of the past ten years 90 percent of the *taxable* income had either been given to charity or paid in taxes. There were two booby traps carefully concealed within this seemingly public-spirited provision which was represented as an encouragement to private charity. I confess I was fooled by them. The first is that it is only 90 percent of the *taxable* income that is counted, and not 90 percent of the real income. By exempting capital gains income and "depletion income," which is not taxed, the proportion of income actually given away can be, and frequently is, only a small fraction of the actual real income. It is therefore especially popular among the oil barons of the Southwest.

The second joker is that by creating "personal foundations" the donor can retain control of those properties that he is apparently giving away and have the income spent in accordance with his wishes and frequently to his profit.

Congressman Wright Patman has unearthed many of the abuses perpetrated by these "foundations." And it is significant that the unlimited charitable deduction ranks alongside the depletion allowance, the fast write-off of drilling and developmental costs, and the capital gains privileges as an important reason why so many men with huge incomes pay small taxes, or none at all.

Men who own their homes are not taxed on the imputed income afforded by that ownership, while the renter receives no credit for the amount that he pays for shelter. A man with a $10,000 salary who lives in a $20,000 house that he owns, and for which, if he did not own it, he would have to pay another person $2,000 a year rent, really has the approximate equivalent of a $12,000 income, but he only pays on $10,000. (For convenience' sake, I am disregarding local property taxes and maintenance costs. These do decrease the tax advantage of the homeowner.) His neighbor across the street who also has a salary of $10,000, but who pays $2,000 rent, is taxed on the *full* $10,000. If we were to preserve uniformity, either the first man's income should be reckoned at $12,000, as was once true in England, or his neighbor should be rated at $8,000. But to adopt this latter method would be to provide that amounts paid in rent should not be taxed as income. This exemption of rent hardly seems equitable.

But, even if justifiable, the inclusion of imputed rent in taxable income hardly seems possible in the near future.

And of course no support could be found to recapture for society some of the increase in bare land values or "locality" values which Allen Manvel has shown probably amounted to $250 billion during the decade from 1956 to 1966, or at the rate of $25 billion a year. This was exclusive of any improvements in or on the soil. It was created by society primarily because of the increase in population. But it was appropriated by certain groups of landowners. This was not in any sense a stealing. But it was also not an earning. As the conservative Thomas Nixon Carver observed long ago it was and is a finding.

Neither is there hope for changing the rule that a husband and wife may split their income for tax purposes. This allows taxation at a lower average rate than if the major share of the income were credited to the financial head of the family, who actually received it. While it does not cost a man and wife twice as much to live as it does a single man, it commonly does cost them more. And while the wife of a well-to-do man costs far more than the $600 of personal exemption that is allowed, nevertheless a distinct tax favor is given to the married men, as it is to homeowners. This tax advantage increases as one moves into higher and higher tax brackets, so that matrimony is relatively more blessed financially for the millionaire than it is for the modest members of the middle and lower economic classes. I cannot believe that the wife of a wealthy man is correspondingly so much better and more socially valuable than the wives of the financially humble.

I began my senatorial career in a quandary, and when I left the quandary was even bigger than when I started. It was this: Can and will the people under the best system of government in the world, and with an able and high-minded Congress, ever be able to protect the public interest in tax matters and enforce equal justice for all?

I must admit that the eighteen years have, on the surface, been disillusioning. We had made a few improvements during that time and may have saved a billion dollars or more a year, but the big loopholes and truckholes remained. Indeed, new ones had been opened, sometimes over our opposition and sometimes, as I have pointed out, without our knowledge. I daresay that there may be still other financial time bombs, presumably concealed in innocent-sounding verbiage, which will turn out to free still more income from taxation. The summing up that Philip Stern gave in his *The Great Treasury Raid* is substantially true today.

> For a raid of its magnitude, the time (high noon) and setting (the United States Treasury, a stone's throw from the White House) showed a breath-taking boldness of design and planning. From out of nowhere, it seemed, they appeared— old people and young, rich and poor, an oil millionaire here, a factory worker there, a real estate tycoon, a working mother, several well-known movie stars, some corporation presidents, even the chairman of a powerful Congressional committee. It

was a mixed lot, all right, that converged on the Treasury Building that high noon. Into the building they strolled, gloriously nonchalant. No one stopped them; not a guard looked up to question them. Quickly and quietly they found their way to the vaults; opened them noiselessly with the special passkeys each had brought with him. Like clockwork, with split-second timing, each went to his appointed spot, picked up a bag and walked out as calmly as he had entered. At the exits the guards sat motionless. At precisely 12:04 it was all over. Each of the "visitors" had vanished into thin air. *So had forty billion dollars from the United States Treasury.*

Despite all our efforts, the brutal fact must be admitted. We have largely failed.

Is the fault then in the structure of our economic life, "in our stars," so to speak, or in ourselves, that so little progress has been made?

It used to be said by some that the trouble with democracy was that the ablest and best-educated men and women in the country did not take part in political affairs, but that if they would only interest themselves more in public matters they would set matters right.

But it has been the extremely able who have inserted these loopholes in the tax laws. The loopholes and even more, the truckholes, are defended against elimination or lessening by other extremely able men. The large hearing room of the Finance Committee seats a hundred and fifty persons. When we considered a tax bill, the room was filled with prosperous lawyers, graduates of great universities and of the top-ranking law schools, whom Assistant Secretary of the Treasury Stanley Surrey once referred to in a burst of awed admiration as "the best minds in the country," all working to hold what they and their clients had and to enlarge it.

One major trouble with our tax system is, therefore, precisely this: that these "best minds" in the country have largely worked to make it what it is. Not more than one out of every hundred citizens actively working on a tax bill is trying to represent the general interest. And in the halls outside the hearing rooms the lobbyists are as thick as flies, while the publicity men and noisemakers are busily at work in Washington and elsewhere. In the halls of academe, erudite professors train their students in the intricacies of the tax code so that their students may succeed in the private practice of law by helping wealthy clients avoid taxes and thus beat the government of the people.

All this raises the question whether this is a fundamental weakness of our democratic system, namely, that the producing and possessing interests are compact, powerful and well organized, while the consuming and nonpossessing classes are busy with other things, and their interests diffused; and that while the people are numerically more numerous, they are collectively weak, ignorant and unorganized. Does it follow that in a conflict between these two groups it is almost invariably the more powerful that wins?

As I watched the struggle and took part in it for nearly two decades, I was struck with the similarity between it and the way the Spaniards were able to take over Mexico, Peru, and indeed all of Latin America, as narrated by William H. Prescott in his two classic histories, the *Conquest of Mexico* and the *Conquest of Peru.*

There were about thirteen million Indians in Mexico whereas there were only about five hundred Spaniards under Cortez. But the Spaniards wore armor, and they had gunpowder and powerful arquebuses, while the Indians were largely unarmed and unprotected. The Spaniards had horses, which gave them mobility, which the Indians did not have. They were, moreover, under tight discipline and moved as one, whereas the Indians were torn by internal dissension and overawed by the proud and arrogant newcomers.

So it sometimes seemed to me in these tax battles. A particular measure would mean millions to a few, but only a few cents to each of the two hundred million Americans. It was hard for the individual citizen to become informed. Even if he knew what was at stake, he was busy earning a living for his family and could not interrupt his work to defend his infinitesimal interest. Leisure, moreover, has its proper claims as well. So only a minute fraction can enlist in the common cause, and they can only do so at great risk to themselves. This in itself is a preventive to action.

James Madison saw this danger to our democracy at the very foundation of our Republic and tried to develop an answer in the tenth essay of *The Federalist*. He thought he had found a partial answer to the peril in the mutual checks and balances that the divergent producing interests, called into being by a national market, would exercise upon each other.

This form of countervailing power is helpful in many fields. But I did not find it to be an adequate protection for the consumers or the small taxpayers. For producers seldom think of consumers, while those with big potential tax bills are commonly not solicitous about the other taxpayers. There is, moreover, a kind of fellow feeling among the powerful that makes it bad form for one group to balk another in a matter in which they are not themselves directly concerned. To do so is to violate the unwritten rules of the predators.

Fortunately, in the history of our Republic, there have generally been some politicians who, at great risk to themselves, have defended the general interest with energy and ability. Such were George Norris of Nebraska, the two Robert La Follettes of Wisconsin, and more recently the beloved Herbert Lehman of New York. Such, I believe, are my friends, Albert Gore of Tennessee and Bill Proxmire of Wisconsin, who have specialized in these very matters. There are many others on the national, state and local levels. Generally, these men in the past were ultimately defeated, but they lasted long enough to make an impression on their times and to win important victories. Their lives and the respect that is later accorded to them after they die (although generally not before) is proof that there is a deep, if unexpressed, hunger on the part of the inarticulate millions for just such defenders.

But political battles cannot be won by solo combat. The days of the knightly tournaments celebrated by Sir Walter Scott in his *Ivanhoe* are over. Modern political struggles, like modern wars, need mass support and an adequate organizing staff if they are to be successful. Where is this support coming from?

The industrial unions, and most conspicuously the United Automobile Workers, have shown the greatest awareness of this need and have, in general, exercised a concerned interest in what may be termed the general welfare. There are various public groups with circumscribed interests that, from time to time, are also helpful. But we would be in a much stronger position if the organization of consumers, now embryonic, were more of a reality than a hope.

When I entered public life, now nearly three decades ago, I assumed in my innocence that man's efforts at just and humane self-government constituted the highest form of secular activity, and that the state was a fitting instrumentality through which man could lead the good life. I had been proud of our national government and thought of it as a friend and not as an enemy, and as something to be served and not exploited.

But it is obvious that this view is not held by a large and influential proportion of the population. As some of their frankest spokesmen have said, they seem to regard the national government as their enemy and as something malign to be hated.

I once heard an eminent public figure declare that it was a man's duty to pay the federal government as little as possible in the way of taxes. Everywhere one finds powerful groups moving in to extract special privileges from our society, and they always seem to be able to attract to their cause skilled lawyers, technical experts, economists, publicity men and public relations practitioners, who then use their brains and wiles to promote the fortunes of their employers. Meanwhile the main mass of the general public and even of the academic profession stand by as mere spectators and allow without protest the power juggernauts to conquer. They behave indeed like so many city spectators who watch crimes being committed without raising a hand to defend the victims or lifting their voices to call the police.

To me this was and is a sign of the disintegration of a society that has lost sight of its common purpose. But to others it is the smart thing to do.

This is what deepened my quandary.

The query is appropriate: Where are the champions of the people? Where are the men, better and more effective than we who have tried and lost, coming from?

I do not know. But I am still an optimist. I cannot believe that the people with all their weaknesses will allow the noble ship of democratic government to be taken over by these well-clad pirates with impeccable credentials. For if they do, there may ultimately be such a disillusion with our form of government as to cause the people in frustration to abandon ship and to allow it to be taken over by a still worse group of tyrants, who will suppress our liberties and shut the gates of mercy on mankind.

2 The Oil Shale Treasure and Attempts to Despoil It

The informed public has only recently become aware of the vast fuel resources in the form of the oil deposits in three Western states.* These are contained in the shale rock in the upper reaches of the valleys of the Green and Grand rivers, which lie on the western slope of the Rockies and stretch from northwestern Colorado into Utah and Wyoming.

In these formations there are, according to the Geological Survey, from 2 trillion to 2 trillion 600 billion barrels of ulti-

* See an article by Chris Welles in *Harper's* for August 1968 which contains a popular version of a detailed analysis originally scheduled for publication in *Life* during the previous winter but which was canceled on the eve of publication.

mately recoverable oil.* This is not a typographical error. There are probably close to 2 trillion barrels of oil in the shale, or 2,000 billion barrels, or 2,000,000 million barrels. This is six times the estimated total known recoverable oil in the entire world, which has been estimated at 360 billion barrels. It is about twenty-five times the total amount of oil which has been extracted throughout the whole history of the American oil industry, and about 600 times as much as our present yearly consumption. At a price of $2.77 a barrel (which is a recent quotation) the resource of 2 trillion barrels would be worth a total of approximately $5.5 trillion. If the reserve amounts to 2.6 trillion barrels, the ultimate gross worth of the entire reserve might run to as high as $7 trillion.

What is almost equally as striking is the fact that about 80 percent of this oil is located in land to which the people of the United States have title, at least for the present. This would come to between 1.6 and 1.7 trillion barrels and to an ultimate value of between $4.5 and $5 trillion.

We ordinarily think of oil as lying far below the surface in underground liquid pools. It is a strange sight, therefore, to see some shale deposits embedded in the heart of the Rockies at from 2,000 to 5,000 feet above the mountain valleys. But the explanation is simple. Some 50 million years ago, this section of the country was covered by a relatively shallow inland lake. Here flourished in profusion a type of microorganism either identical with or closely similar to the plankton, which is even now the ultimate source of nutriment in the sea as chlorophyll is upon the land, and which is commonly supposed to be the basic source of liquid oil, whether under land or under the bed of the sea. As these organisms fell to the bottom of the shallow lake, they became covered with and embedded in the other matter at the bottom. This hardened into a

* Interim Report of the Oil Shale Advisory Board, February 1965, p. 2. A recent report by the Interior Department reduces this estimate somewhat.

rock form. When the lake began to dry up, this process was intensified. The oil-impregnated matter was very deep at the center. Then came the upthrust, from geologic causes, of the earth from the plain. This pushed what we now call the Rockies several thousands of feet into the sky and in the process raised some of the oil-impregnated matter or shale into the heart of the mountain structure. After one has had some experience, one can roughly identify these layers of oil shale or oil marl, which run in depth from a few feet to nearly a quarter of a mile. As one moves through the western slope of the Colorado Rockies, there it is, towering above one and observable to even a moderately trained eye. But the oil shale also lies below the surface as well as on the heights. In some of the valleys it may be as much as a thousand or more feet down.

The shale, of course, is of widely varying richness. In the Piceance Valley and Rio Blanco County, for example, the vein will be as deep as 1,200 feet while the oil will run from 30 or 35 gallons or more to the ton. There will be millions of dollars' worth of oil below the surface of an acre. On the outskirts of the deposits the vein will be far more shallow, while the oil content may not exceed 5 to 10 gallons to the ton.

This variation in the thickness of the veins of oil shale naturally limits the amount of the deposit that it is economically feasible to develop. The Bureau of Mines developed an experimental plant at Anvil Points near Rifle, Colorado, for nearly a decade, from 1947 to 1956. Here the bureau developed the mining, crushing, and retorting processes. It was, however, closed down by the Eisenhower Administration along with a sister plant at Louisiana, Missouri, designed to extract oil from bituminous coal. It is not known what the results in terms of actual cost were. It is believed that the Anvil Points plant had approached a profitable breakthrough when the established oil industries wanted it stopped, lest it threaten to replace their own sources of supply.

Work was resumed under the Kennedy Administration, when the Anvil Points facility was leased without charge to a research foundation of the Colorado School of Mines. This in turn subleased it to a consortium headed by Mobil Oil, which also included five other oil companies: Humble (a Standard Oil subsidiary), Continental, Pan American, Phillips and Sinclair. The statistics on production costs were closely guarded by this consortium and the Bureau of Mines. But the companies were sufficiently encouraged by their early experience to embark on the second phase of their program and to drive a further horizontal tunnel on a larger scale into the middle of the mountain and widen the working faces from which the shale or marl is being extracted. More recently some solid cost figures have been released.

A few years ago additional experimental work was also being carried out in the western Rockies by the Union Oil Company of California. This was however discontinued some years back. Some charge that the work was only stopped after Union had been given a slice of the oil from the Persian Gulf by the American firms operating in that area.

The Oil Shale Company (Tosco), owned originally by Standard Oil of Ohio (Sohio) and the Cleveland Cliffs Corporation of Cleveland, is carrying on work somewhat parallel to that conducted at the neighboring facility at Anvil Points. High security is enforced at this plant and, as I found by a personal visit, visitors are not allowed even to catch sight of the plant, although enterprising reporters have viewed it from the air. It probably uses the same basic mining and crushing process, but possibly a different method of retorting. Here again, no one knows what the cost figures actually are. They may threaten the conventional methods and sources.

From inspecting the Anvil Points plant and from observing the terrain surrounding the operation at Tosco, it is apparent that the present logistic problems under the mining and crushing process are severe. The mining of the shale from within the mountain is at a distance of 5.2 miles from the processing complex at the Anvil Points plant and at least two thousand feet above it. The rock, after being mined by modern methods within the mountain * from horizontal shafts, is transported by truck down a series of sharply sloping switchbacks to where it is successively crushed laterally, then retorted by the gas-combustion method developed by the Bureau of Mines † and finally given rough refining. It is understood that previously the Bureau of Mines had virtually reached the point of extracting approximately 30 gallons to the ton of shale, or roughly seven-tenths of a barrel. It is also believed that the optimum daily output of a plant using substantially this method would be 50,000 barrels. This would mean that such a plant would have to have a daily input of about 70,000 tons of shale (i.e., $50,000 \times {}^{10}\!/_7 = 71,400$).

The difficulties and cost of moving this volume of rock such a distance and down such a slope are obvious. If the crushing plant could either be located inside the mine itself or close to it, these costs could be greatly reduced and the practicality of the project enhanced. It may be impossible, however, to place the retorts inside the mines because of their height. If so, they should be as close to the mines as possible. Certainly the costly and laborious trucking should be reduced to the greatest degree possible and gravity should be used to move the shale to and from the crusher wherever practicable. The crude oil from the retorts can of course be pumped for further refining through pipes.

* *Oil Shale Mining, Rifle, Colorado, 1944–56*, by J. H. East and E. D. Gardner, Bulletin 611, Bureau of Mines.
† For an explanation of this method, see *Development of the Bureau of Mines; Gas-Combustion Oil Shale Retorting Process* by Matzids, Dannenberg, Ruard, Philips, Lankford and Guthrie. Bulletin 635, Bureau of Mines, 1966, 199 pp.

If deep mining is carried on below the surface of the valleys, the processes will largely depend on how far down the oil shale lies and how thick the vein is. The open-pit method is now used for iron ore on the Mesabi range, for copper at the Bingham mine in Utah and also in Arizona and for the strip mining of coal. It can be used here if the oil shale lies within a manageable distance from the surface. If it is far underground, the whole process will be more complicated, expensive and perhaps impossible. The four consecutive steps of mining, crushing, retorting and refining will still have to be carried out under this method, but the location of each of these processes will vary according to the physical circumstances.

Some engineers have estimated that it would not be economically practicable to develop reserves where there are fewer than 15 gallons of oil per ton of shale and where the deposits are less than 15 or 20 feet deep. They therefore estimate that the presently feasible reserves amount not to 2 trillion barrels, but to no more than 300 to 360 billion barrels. Even if this lower estimate were to be true, the actual extent of the commercially available reserves would still be unbelievably vast. It would be equal to the total presently known reserves of the entire world and about one hundred times our present yearly consumption. Moreover, as technology improves and costs are lowered, a larger and larger quantity of the reserves will become economically feasible. It will, however, be very difficult to mine the underground reserves requiring vertical shafts instead of the horizontal shafts now used at Anvil Points.

In addition to the oil, some of the shale deposits also include dawsonite, from which aluminum can be made but which is also a sodium compound, and nahcolite (sodium bicarbonate). Formerly there were no hard estimates of the probable quantities of these minerals, but a recent report of the Department of the Interior * estimates that in 235 square

* Oil Shale Prospects in Colorado, Utah and Wyoming, p. 2.

1459549

miles in the Piceance Basin there are 27 billion tons of
dawsonite containing slightly over 9 billion tons of alumina.
There are also tremendous quantities of soda ash.

To the degree that these are mixed with the oil shale, it
probably would only be feasible to develop them commercially
as a by-product of the oil-extraction process. Their presence
introduces legal complications which recent claimants have
tried to take advantage of but which, under the Mineral Leasing Act of 1920, can also be used to protect the public interest.

An important difficulty of the crushing process is that of
disposing of the residue. With rock yielding 30 gallons to the
ton, the total weight of the extracted oil would come to 225
pounds to the ton, while at 20 gallons the extracted oil would
come to 150 pounds. This would leave a residue from each ton
of from 1,775 to 1,850 pounds, or not far from nine-tenths of a
ton. We have estimated that a plant of optimum size would
need an input of approximately 70,000 tons of shale a day,
and this would mean that the daily residue under these conditions would be not far from 63,000 tons, or about 23 million
tons a year. This quantity would be staggering in itself, but
when we consider that this is for only one plant and that the
total quantity would ultimately be many times this, we can
form some idea of the magnitude of the problem. Furthermore,
it is estimated by some that the amount of cubic space required by the residual is approximately 1.3 times greater than
that of the more compact shale. This would make the residue
the equivalent in space of a little over 80,000 tons a day per
plant, or close to 30 million tons a year. Even if this residue
were put back in the mine, starting at the lowest levels, as is
proposed for the lateral shafts on the mountain sides, it would
probably overflow the space created by mining by not far
from a seventh. Even these dumps would create a severe problem. They would at best disfigure the marvelously beautiful
mountain sides and valleys of the Rockies. The falling rains and
melted snows would almost inevitably wash chemicals into

the streams and rivers that would probably be poisonous to fish and spread the damage hundreds of miles downstream.

All this would be compounded were all the residue, as some advocate, to be dumped into the valleys. The area would then be in danger of being turned into a region of hideous strip mines. The easy claims of the developers that these dangers can be controlled by proper chemical and engineering treatment need to be carefully checked before the dangers can be dismissed.

The crushing method would also require a huge amount of capital. Thus it was estimated that an investment of $2,000 is needed for each barrel of oil produced daily. A plant with a capacity of 50,000 barrels would therefore call for an investment of around $100 million.* When it is remembered that the area any one plant could serve is necessarily limited by the difficulties of moving the shale, and that consequently many plants will be needed to develop the field, it becomes evident that a huge investment of capital will be required. This will be far beyond the resources of the small operators and "wild-catters." From the very start, therefore, the big operators will dominate both the mining and the crushing-retorting phases of the process.

The second way of extracting oil from the shale is the so-called *in situ* method. This consists of injecting intense heat, whether gaseous, scalding steam or nuclear energy, into a deep well and then forcing it through the shale. Once it reaches 900° Fahrenheit, the heat decomposes the organic matter into three parts: oil (approximately two-thirds), gas (one-tenth) and coke (one-fourth). The coke and gas can then be relied upon to furnish additional heat during the later

---

* This was also the estimate of Captain Howard Moore, U.S.N., before the Senate Anti-Monopoly Committee, February 21, 1967. See pp. 80, 86 and 158. Apparently the Tosco group has made somewhat similar estimates. More recent estimates fix the probable cost at a higher figure of around $2,500 per ton.

cumulative stages of the process. This method is therefore like that of gas-combustion now used in the retorts. Once started, it feeds on itself and is therefore self-generating.

Once the oil has been separated from the shale, it will then flow into an underground pool from which it can be pumped out for retorting and refining through another well. It can then be pumped from the surface to refineries for further processing.

The *in situ* method has been used in Scotland and Scandinavia with some degree of success and the Bureau of Mines has experimented with this process at its plant in Laramie, Wyoming. A trial run of this method is scheduled in the Colorado area by private interests.*

A new and daring development of this process is to use atomic or nuclear energy, thus providing great heat and, at the same time, fracturing the shale to permit a more rapid and complete flow of the viscous oil into the underground pool. It is known that the Atomic Energy Commission has been conducting experiments in this field at its Livermore, California, installation as part of its Operation Bronco, but no information has been given out about results.

It is obvious that if the *in situ* method can be successfully and economically completed, it will have tremendous advantages over the conventional mining and crushing process. It will obviously eliminate the problems of mining and moving and disposing of the huge quantities of rock involved in the conventional method. By not disturbing the surface of the area, it will do no damage to the scenery, and will not fill the valleys with waste. An engineer connected with the Atomic Energy Commission has estimated that production costs could be as low as 30 cents a barrel, but this has been sharply challenged by advocates of the conventional method. A recent

* For a description of the process, see H. W. Sohne and H. C. Carpenter, "In Situ Oil Shale Retorting," *Chemical Engineering Progress,* Vol. 62, August 1966, pp. 75–78.

report of the Interior Department fixes the initial costs at between $3 and $4 a barrel and the ultimate costs at somewhere
between $1.25 and $1.40 a barrel. Moreover, it should greatly
diminish the amount of capital required by the three stages
of mining, crushing and retorting. It may even decrease the
costs of the first refining. This would make more competition
in the ultimate refining possible, and it would also require
co-operation between the Atomic Energy Commission and any
private corporation that might become involved in the work.

We may therefore shortly see technical improvements that
will remove many of the difficulties now looming so large with
the mining and crushing method. The moral would seem to
be that we should push experimental work under the *in situ*
process and that we should use not only intensely hot steam
but also the nuclear energy process. Operation Bronco should
therefore be vigorously pursued.

I made an exploratory trip to the oil shale lands of Colorado
during the early summer of 1967 in order to see the physical
layout of the deposits and to form an idea of the technical
problems of production. In my innocence, I had assumed that
the title of the government to its lands was clear and un-
clouded. To my surprise I found that this was not so. In the
first place, a great many private claims had been filed for oil
on government-owned oil shale land immediately after World
War I under the Mining Law of 1872.

Congress had then tried in February 1920 to check this
alienation of the publicly owned lands which contained oil, oil
shale, coal, sodium, phosphate and other mineral products. Instead of giving away these lands to private claimants, as had
been done by the Mining Law of 1872,* the new act provided
instead for leasing with the title of ownership still retained by

* U.S. Code, Title 30. Paragraphs 21–72. Act of May 10, 1872, Chapter
152.

the government.* After the terms of the lease had been mutually agreed upon by the government and the private parties, then the latter could start mining with title to the product assured, but not to the land.

The new Mineral Leasing Act, however, contained a "grandfather" clause which legalized all filings which had been made on these minerals before the date of its passage, namely, February 25, 1920. About 345,000 acres were granted to private parties under 2,300 claims during the next 40 years. Herein lies a graphic story, the full truth of which is not yet known.

As it turned out, these 1918–19 filings had primarily been where the oil shale was on or close to the surface and visible to the eye. Later it was discovered that they were largely on the outskirts of the major deposits. The really deep and thick deposits were farther back at the centers of the original lakes and hence now on the higher slopes of the Rockies. They were also often many hundreds of feet below the surface. These fortunately were often not filed on during the 1918–19 rush of claims. But as we shall see they furnished the prize for which private interests contended from 1965 to February 1967, when they were filed on in a profuse rush of claims under the original Mining Law of 1872 on the grounds that they contained dawsonite, a compound from which alumina can be derived. This, as we shall see, was claimed as a mineral outside of the Leasing Act of 1920. The Leasing Act had also given to the Secretary of the Interior the power to withdraw such lands from filing.

The law of 1872, passed in the days of the small-scale individual prospector, had made very few demands upon the claimants:

1. They had to stake out the four corners of their placer claim, which could amount to 160 acres if there were as

* U.S. Code, Title 30. Paragraphs 181–194. Act of February 25, 1920, Chapter 85.

many as eight persons in whose name the claim was filed.
2. The original claim had to be filed in the county where the location had been staked out. There was no centralized record of these claims.
3. There must have been an actual discovery of the minerals claimed, sufficient (as it was later interpreted) to convince a "prudent" man that it was practicable to try to extract them.
4. Before the claim was finally granted or "patented" by the government, the claimant must give evidence of his earnestness by spending at least $500 over a five-year period to develop each claim of 160 acres. This could be either at the rate of $100 a year for five years or the whole amount in one year. Expenditures on access roads could be included in the developmental costs.
5. Upon meeting these conditions, the lands in question would be transferred by the government to the approved claimant upon payment of $2.50 an acre.

There was unfortunately no limit in the original Mineral Act of 1872 to the number of claims any one group could file. It was apparently taken for granted that only individuals would stake out and file claims, and that this in itself would limit the size of any one set of claims. The rest of the country was not greatly interested in the field of mining law and this feature of the 1872 act has never been amended.

A considerable degree of laxness in the administration of the 1872 act developed over the years. Since the filings of the original claims were made in the courthouses of the thinly settled mining counties, the federal government had no central record of what claims had been filed and was not in a position to challenge the claimants as to whether (a) the corners of the claim had actually been staked out, or (b) whether actual evidence had been physically presented that a "discovery" of the minerals had been made. Since the county officials seldom, if ever, made such a challenge, it was hard for the government to prove that these conditions had not been met. The mere assertions of the claimants came more and more to be accepted at face value, both by the courts and by the government. Moreover, even the provision that $500 must be expended in improvements and developments within a five-year period came to be something of a dead letter. The burden of proof was thrown completely upon the government to show that the sums had not been expended, and in view of the isolation of the claims this was very hard to do. The Supreme Court moreover ruled that failure to perform this assessment work gave the government no right of forfeiture.

The legal position of the government was still further weakened by a series of court decisions beginning in the 1930's and extending as late as 1966. These prevented the government from refusing to "patent" or grant a claim because of the nonperformance of the supposed requirements. It is difficult to explain these decisions on logical grounds. The human reasons may have been a varied combination of factors. The claimants possessed great economic and political power. There was a failure of government officials to defend adequately the rights of the public and, finally, there was a general resentment in the mining states toward the federal government because it, and not the states, owned the land in question, and a feeling that Washington was standing in the way of the development of the area and thus holding back the prosperity of the region.

There was, therefore, a built-in regional bias against any vigorous enforcement of the public's rights and in favor of the claimants, however spurious their claims. When the federal government, because of private pressure, either acquiesced in these grants or put up very weak resistance to them, the issue was really allowed to go by default. During the 1920's the Interior Department was itself weak.

Despite warnings issued in 1930 by Ralph S. Kelley, head of the Denver branch of the General Land Office, that there had been widespread alienation of the public lands under the 1918–19 filings,* this fact tended to be neglected.

When the Advisory Commission on Oil Shale reported in 1965 that perhaps 20 percent of the oil shale lands were in private hands, few raised the question as to how they got that way. When I went through the area, the common explanation was that these lands had been acquired from homesteaders and this statement continued to be made by the Interior Department. Some had been obtained in this fashion but, as a recent analysis finally prepared by Interior has shown,† the majority of these lands had been obtained because the Interior Department in years past had allowed claims to be finally approved and patented without any serious questioning as to whether the conditions laid down by the 1872 law had been observed. Some may have been well founded but others were not. In all, no less than 264.1 million acres had been alienated in this manner in Colorado alone, involving 263 successful applications for patents. ‡ A large number of these were issued when Albert Fall was Secretary of the Interior and these alienations amounted to approximately 46,000 acres.§ But they did not stop with Secretary Fall's departure from public office. There were also many patents issued during the latter part of 1924 and also 1925, and some as late as 1928–31. || Only a few were granted under Secretary Ickes, who was alert to the

* See the series of articles by Mr. Kelley in the New York *World* from October 6 to 19, 1930. In particular the Freeman-Summers Midwest Oil Refining Co. and the Lyons cases deserve study.

† See *Prospects for Oil Shale Development*, p. 17.

‡ See an unpublished manuscript, "Oil Shale Patents, Colorado," dated March 7, 1967. 24 pp.

§ Amongst the patents issued from 1921 to 1925 were those to the Federal Shale Oil Company, Bruce and Rea Eaton, Roderick Burnham, Renwick Ralston, Leland Murshall, Delos Potter, and Columbia Oil Shale. During this period E. C. Finney was the Assistant Secretary of the Interior and continued in that office for many years.

|| Among these later patentees were Lipman P. Lyons, Delos Potter, Denver Oil Shale Company, H. G. Slusser, Virginia-Colorado Co.

danger but who had been handicapped by the decision of the Supreme Court in the Virginia-Colorado case.

During the latter part of the forties, the tempo of approvals picked up with patents being granted on close to 30,000 acres. From 1953 through 1956 a further rush of patents was also granted.* It is a pleasure to record that under Secretary Udall there is no record of a single patent being granted.

While political comparisons may seem odious, it is also a fact that of the 264,000 acres in Colorado which were allowed to go into private hands over this period of nearly half a century, approximately 210,500 acres were transferred during the 20 years of Republican Administrations and 53,500 in the 26 years of Democratic rule up to March of 1967. There were approximately 80,000 more acres in Utah and Wyoming which were given away in this fashion during the years 1920–60.

By 1965, therefore, when the Advisory Committee on Oil Shale made its report, some 15 to 20 percent of the shale lands were privately owned. But the drive for private appropriation of the lands picked up steam. In the first place, the federal district court handed down a decision that opened the way to recognizing pre-1920 claims, which were nearly a half century old and upon which little or no work had been done. Here the government's case had originally been poorly presented, by arguing that the Interior had a precedent in withholding the land from transfer rather than pointing out that the claimants had slept on their alleged rights for decades until speculators, presumably from the big companies, had bought up the claims. It did not seem, moreover, that the government had adequately challenged the alleged fact of there being any actual "discovery" of oil, particularly in veins lying far underneath the surface.

This was bad enough. For unless finally reversed by a higher

* Amongst the successful were many claims of Delos D. Potter and of his estate and some by A. H. Powell, Barney Whately, and others.

court, the decision opened up for private appropriation further large areas of public lands that had previously been thought safe.

But worse was to come. There were rumors that there had been recent extensive private filings of claims for minerals such as dawsonite, nahcolite, and silver on lands not previously filed upon and believed to be extremely rich in shale oil. Two men, Eugene Cervi of *Cervi's Rocky Mountain Journal* of Denver, and a fighting young editor, J. R. Freeman of the *Farmer and Miner* of Frederick, Colorado, were especially active in calling the attention of the public to what they believed was going on.

I therefore decided to visit two of the most important oil counties, Garfield and Rio Blanco, and did so in July 1967 in company with a respected Denver attorney, Daniel Lynch, a regent of the University of Colorado, and Douglas Bradley, an Oxford graduate and a reporter on *Cervi's Rocky Mountain Journal*. We visited the offices of the respective clerks and recorders of these counties at Glenwood Springs and Meeker, where we examined the volumes containing the filings. We discovered that mineral claims had been filed for almost half of the entire Rio Blanco County (which contains most of the rich Piceance Valley) and that these covered most of the shale lands. This was confirmed by a map that had been prepared by Robert White, who ran the local abstract office.* We also found that private mineral claims had also been filed on a large proportion of shale lands in Garfield County where the Anvil Points and Tosco operations are located.

We were particularly startled by the large number of claims filed by Merle Zweifel of Shawnee, Oklahoma. When he did so he always included two women members of his

---

* There was some overlap with the pre-1920 claims in the southern part of the county but most of the Zweifel filings were on land not previously claimed and especially rich in deep-lying shale.

family, Bonnie E. and Maude H. Zweifel, and he would also include five other associates to make a total of eight. Since an individual is permitted, under the placer mining claims, to file on a maximum of only 20 acres, this made it possible for him to file on 160 acres, or a quarter section, on any one placer claim. In Garfield County I found Zweifel had filed no fewer than 338 claims in a little over a year.* These, however, were mostly on 80-acre lots; they totaled over 26,000 acres. The filing figures in Rio Blanco County were almost astronomical. Here the mere indexing of the claims filed by the Zweifel group filled 79 pages of the master record book. In all, he entered in this county 2,578 mineral placer claims. These were generally for a full quarter section, and hence probably covered about 400,000 acres (about 600 square miles).† A list of these filings was deposited with the Senate Interior Committee.

There were other groups that had filed on these lands, of which perhaps the most important was headed by Frank G. Cooley, the county attorney of Rio Blanco County.‡

Mr. Zweifel seems to be a most expansive and frank man, and in a letter dated June 26, 1967, to J. R. Freeman, the brave local editor, he has stated that he has recently filed over "20,000 claims" covering approximately "4 million acres." § Just who is behind Zweifel's activities and what his motives are is something of a mystery. In a telephone interview with *Cervi's Rocky Mountain Journal,* he is said to have admitted that he had represented three big oil companies, but claimed that in most cases he had been acting for thousands of small investors.

That there may be big money behind Zweifel is indicated by the expense to which he has already gone and the addi-

* See Volumes 378, 381 and 382 of the Garfield County Records.
† See Volumes 271–279 and 281–284 of the Rio Blanco County Records.
‡ *Cervi's Rocky Mountain Journal* for July 19, 1967, p. 2, gives the names of some of the other filers.
§ Letter from Zweifel to Freeman, 6/26/67. He also stated that "Tosco and Kaiser have filed about 1,000 claims, I would estimate" and in a disarming fashion he wrote, *"Ramparts* accused me of stealing four million acres, which is *not quite true."* (My italics.)

tional amounts he will be forced to spend before his claims
can be finally approved and patented by the government. His
personal expenses incurred in such wholesale filings have in
the first place been large. In addition he must pay appreciable filing fees to each county. And before the claims
can be finally validated and patented the claimant must
swear, as I have stated, that he has spent $500 in developing
each claim. If Zweifel has made 20,000 filings, the total cost
for this item alone, if not waived, would be $10 million. In
Rio Blanco and Garfield Counties this would amount to over
$1.4 million on the specific claims filed. Some claim Zweifel
has not been operating for the big oilmen but for himself and
a series of small speculators. In January 1967, Secretary Udall
stopped the filings. He has been criticized by some for not
having done so earlier.

It should be remembered that Zweifel and others have been
filing mineral rather than oil claims, since the latter were
barred in this area under President Hoover by Secretary of
the Interior Ray Lyman Wilber, in order to head off the possibility of another Teapot Dome. But since the dawsonite,
nahcolite and possibly silver are inextricably combined in the
rocks with the oil, with the mining and crushing process it is
virtually impossible to extract one without affecting the other.
A clue to a possible motive is given by affidavits inserted by
Zweifel at several points in the county records, in which he
asserts that the government or persons to whom it leases may
not extract oil from the shale without his consent and that of
his co-claimants.* This suggests that a possible motive may be
to delay the production of the oil until terms satisfactory to
Zweifel or his principals could be obtained from the government. Zweifel gave some confirmation to this surmise when
he told *Cervi's Journal:* "What we are trying to do is to break

* See the clause inserted in a Garfield County parcel of 3,680 acres,
printed in *Cervi's Rocky Mountain Journal,* July 19, 1967, p. 20.

the stranglehold on oil shale. We are going out on a limb to challenge the government. We are trying to force the federal government to work out a proposal to mine our minerals in association with oil shale production." *

Some believe that certain oil companies are behind Zweifel and are using his claims to prevent any oil shale development until it is convenient for them to engage in it. The loss of Middle Eastern or Venezuelan oil would, for example, accelerate such a development, as would the growing exhaustion of the domestic fields and further technical progress in the methods of extracting oil from the shale. In short, the claims could be used to hold back developments until the oil companies are ready. If the companies, moreover, were to take over the mineral claims from Zweifel, it would obviously strengthen them in their negotiations with the government.

There are two requirements under the Mineral Act of 1872 that may turn out to be the undoing of Zweifel and other recent claimants. These are the provisions that as a warning to others the four corners of each claim must be staked out and marked by the claimants at the time they are located and that specimens of the minerals found on each claim must also be submitted as proof of legitimate discovery. Since each claimant is required to mention the date on which a given claim was "located," we can get circumstantial evidence as to whether or not this was actually performed. The records show that the claims were filed in batches of thirty or so on any given day. Each one was for 160 acres or a quarter of a square mile. Thus in Rio Blanco, Zweifel filed 39 claims on November 30, 1966, and 30 on December 7. It is obvious that it would have been virtually impossible for him to have physically covered in the high Rockies the four corners of each of the claims in a single day as stated, much less to have kept this same gait up day after day, week after week, month

* *Ibid.*, p. 2.

after month. Moreover, many of these claims were alleged to have been "located" and hence staked on winter days such as January 23 when the Rockies were impassable. The circumstantial evidence, therefore, is strong that even this minimum condition of the 1872 Mining Law was not really complied with. In addition, can evidence be produced that the claimants submitted mineral specimens at the time to justify their claims of discovery? Where the shale is deep below the surface, how could this be done?

Upon my return from the inspection trip, I immediately reported to Secretary Udall what I had found and urged him to send a trusted assistant to verify my evidence and then, if found valid, to file suit to invalidate the Zweifel and other claims. I also discussed the matter with Solicitor Barry of the Interior Department and showed him the xeroxed copy of the master file of Zweifel's claims in Rio Blanco County. I pointed out that to fight these claims one by one, as some government attorneys wanted, would take forever and a day, since there were thousands of them scattered over the whole area. In the meantime Zweifel and others would go unchallenged on the overwhelming mass of the filings and resources. I therefore urged that a mass attack be made upon the whole set of filings. In each case I followed up the conversations with detailed memoranda and I also urged this in testimony before the Senate Interior Committee in September.

It seemed impossible to me that Zweifel and others had performed the minimum technical requirements of staking and discovering on the site of the claims the actual minerals of dawsonite, nahcolite, silver, etc. Any fraud that may have been committed would have been in the first instance against the counties rather than the federal government. The ultimate loser, however, would be the national government as the owner of the oil-impregnated shale. The counties were in a sense acting as the agents of the federal government.

Furthermore, regardless of the fact that the century-old Mining Law was almost incredibly loose in not limiting the number of claims that any one person could file, it was certainly never intended to make possible a wholesale grabbing of the public domain. It was intended instead to apply to the individual prospector who would largely mine his claim by hand labor. It was never intended to permit billions and possibly trillions of dollars of natural resources to be alienated for the benefit of a few wealthy and powerful individuals and corporations. Since equity should lie at the basis of law, I felt that the Interior Department should use every legitimate means to protect this enormously valuable resource for the public, and to do so quickly and effectively. This would require a mighty effort and great expense. But the enormous stakes would justify the effort.

I tried to point out, both to the officials of the department and to the Senate Interior Committee, that with the passage of time it would be increasingly hard to prove that the four corners of each claim had not been staked out. Zweifel and others could always counter by saying that the stakes and notices had become victims of time and the weather. It would also be harder to prove that no tangible evidence of actual discovery had been produced before the county recorders, who could also plead faulty memory.

Solicitor Frank Barry of the Interior Department replied that he could not agree to a mass or wholesale attack on the Zweifel claims, since there was always the chance that some of them were legitimate. He wanted instead to proceed case by case.

The Assistant Attorney General in charge of the public lands, in a letter to Mr. Freeman in May 1966, did not commit himself on whether action should or should not be taken but did not mention any possible illegality in Zweifel's action.

There the legal matter rested as of the winter of 1968. Great issues were at stake. I had every confidence in Secretary Udall, whom I regard as an able and devoted public servant. But though I knew how strong were the subterranean forces that encompassed him, I also knew how every good public servant needs understanding and support from the public if he is to protect the general interest. I can only say that it would be unconscionable if we were to allow this great natural resource, which could do so much for the people of this nation, to slip through our fingers and into the hands of the powerful few.

We need, therefore, not only to clear up the titles to the oil shale lands, as Secretary Udall has properly stated, but to strive aggressively to retain them in public ownership. In order to handle the more than 20,000 claims, the services of a large staff of attorneys and mining engineers will be required. The costs may run well over 30 or 40 millions of dollars. But the stakes are far greater than this, and time is of the essence before the trail gets cold and the evidence disappears.

The legal situation is grave and the amounts at issue unbelievably huge. Our government is like Gulliver tied down by such a multitude of tiny legal threads as apparently to immobilize it. I am afraid that only by an heroic effort can Uncle Sam, the modern Gulliver, break the bonds and recapture his rightful heritage, and yet I believe that the ultimate justice of the cause is such that if it is properly and vigorously advanced, it can be won. The cynics will say that this is an unrealistic hope and that the balance of forces in the country will doom the public interest.

For although the enormous value of the resources was well understood by the oil and mining interests, it was still virtually unknown to the general public. Moreover, the very hugeness of the amounts involved tends to numb the mind and drug the will. It gives to the main mass of citizens a feeling of individual helplessness in the face of gigantic issues and forces.

This general feeling of apprehension is heightened by our past record of alienating and giving away our great natural resources. The record of Congress was indelibly stained by the huge grants of land it made to the transcontinental railways in the decades following the Civil War. Similarly, Congress and the Interior Department prior to 1902 permitted the wealthy timber thieves to take over most of our great forests, which were originally owned by the national government.

In our time we have also seen Congress, in the Communications Act, give the airwaves to private radio and television networks and stations, and to do so without compensation. These are now the chief assets of these private broadcasters and telecasters. They are worth billions of dollars and will be worth more. And they give to their owners tremendous influence over the formation of public taste and political opinion.

But we should also not forget Teapot Dome, Elk Hills and the offshore oil question, where the public interest finally triumphed against seemingly insuperable odds. The alienation of the Teapot Dome and Elk Hills liquid oil reserves was plotted during the campaign of 1920 and was to have been consummated in the administration of Warren G. Harding. The initial steps were, indeed, taken, and the final betrayal was only prevented by a few alert and public-spirited newspapermen and heroic Senators. The spotlight was first thrown on the transaction by a brave young reporter by the name of Clinton P. Anderson, now the senior Senator from New Mexico, and his courageous editor, Carl Magee. The St. Louis *Post-Dispatch* and its Washington correspondent, Paul Y. Anderson, then took up the battle and the latter interested three fearless Senators, Tom Walsh and Burton K. Wheeler of Montana, and Robert M. La Follette, Sr. of Wisconsin. Over the opposition of the financial, political, and newspaper establishment, these men finally exposed the shameful shenanigans and saved the oil fields for the people.

The struggle over offshore oil, in the Gulf of Mexico and

off the coast of California, also shows that the public does not always lose out. This battle was started in the forties by powerful oil interests and by a few states. The Supreme Court had properly ruled that the right to the oil below the floor of the ocean, from the low-water mark out to the three-mile limit, belonged to the national government. Thus, they upheld Secretary Harold L. Ickes, who had been defending the public interest. This seemed to me sound, both under international law and from the fact that the national government, not the states, had the obligation to police and protect those waters. But the big oil interests and a number of states sponsored congressional legislation to reverse this ruling and to give these rights to the states. Senator Lister Hill of Alabama and I felt that this was wrong and that the title should continue to rest with the national government. Senator Hill devised the happy slogan of "oil for the lamps of learning." He proposed that the federal revenues obtained from the oil by royalties and leases should be used to provide aid to the states for primary and secondary education. This brought us some added support, but despite a running parliamentary battle of nearly a month, we were faced with complete and overwhelming defeat.

Then we discovered that the proposed legislation not only granted to the states the right to the oil and gas out to the three-mile limit and, in the case of Texas, to the three-league limit (10½ miles), but also to the very edge of the continental shelf itself. In the Gulf of Mexico, where the waters, because of alluvial deposits washed down over millions of years from the Mississippi basin, are relatively shallow, this was from 75 to 150 miles offshore. No one had ever claimed that these rights belonged to the states, and when we forced Senator Cordon, the sponsor of the measure, to admit the full extent of his bill, there was a sharp revulsion against this provision both in the Senate and in the press gallery. After some discussion, the Senator temporarily left the floor for lunch and when he returned after a few hours of rest and meditation he threw in the sponge and agreed to grant title to the deposits beyond the three-mile and three-league limit to the national government. I suppose that even here there might be some question as to whether or not under international law our national government could actually claim such a title, but there was no rival international authority in being, and we were happy to obtain this concession.

Neither we nor the sponsors of the legislation, however, felt at the time that this concession was particularly important, since we all thought that the overwhelming proportion of the oil would be within the fixed offshore limits of three miles and three leagues, for it was here that the wells had been sunk. It is both ironical and fortunate that the actual developments have shown that the major reserves lie outside these limits. The technical methods that have been developed for drilling wells in relatively deep water have enabled the oil operators to drill much farther out. While there are still disputes as to where "the shore" begins, the federal government had received, up to 1967, a little over $1.1 billion in rents, royalties and bonuses, while another $810 million then in escrow will probably ultimately revert to it. In addition, bids were opened in June 1967 on the leasing rights to additional underwater acreage off the Louisiana coast. The highest bids came to a total of more than $500 million. Additional acreage will also be shortly opened for further competitive bidding.

Thus we have already saved approximately $2½ billion for the nation, and over the course of the years this will probably be multiplied many times as additional royalties come in. The national government, moreover, has the legal title to other precious mineral rights in the sea that now are only dimly understood.

And so it was by a fortunate series of accidents, including an unintentionally overheard conversation, that we averted a gigantic legalized theft of public rights. Horace Walpole, the eighteenth-century English writer would have called this an example of what he termed "serendipity"—obtaining by chance an unintentional and fortunate windfall while pursuing another and very different purpose.

But we cannot expect to be so accidentally lucky in the present instance. The big oil interests are fully aware of the tremendous stakes involved, while the public interest is still both flickering and diffused. Our victory in the case of offshore oil indicates, however, that with adequate support the public interest can triumph.

Every citizen should know that he now owns from 8,500 to 10,000 barrels of this oil, worth from 20 to 25 thousand dollars. He also owns large quantities of aluminum and sodium. He should be on guard against efforts to alienate this property of his. These vast resources give us three great opportunities. In the first place, they can supplement our present conventional oil reserves, from which we have apparently skimmed off the richer portions on the American mainland. Since the rich reserves around the Persian Gulf are presently in great danger of being taken over by a combination of Russia and the militant Arab states, this reserve may be needed much more quickly than we had believed. We do have, however, the offshore reserves of the Gulf of Mexico and the California coast.

Secondly, this immense wealth now owned by all the people in the United States can, if appropriate steps are taken, be preserved in public ownership and kept under public control. This can be combined with the private operation of a large part of mining, extraction and marketing processes under a suitable system of co-operation between the government and private industry.

Finally, if we make the proper decisions, these concentrated resources can be efficiently used in meeting vital human and social needs that would otherwise be largely neglected.

Committees of citizens interested in protecting the public interest on specific issues have been and are of great service. Thus, the numerous conservation groups have checked many depredations and have helped to develop our national and local parks. They furnish the driving force for progressive legislation and help hard-pressed public servants who feel surrounded by predators. Such a group is needed to protect this public interest in oil shale. I have, therefore, proposed that a citizens' watch dog committee on oil shale be organized to help protect the public interest. As an indication of the types of men I would like to see serve on such a committee, I might suggest Senators Lee Metcalf of Montana, Philip Hart of Michigan and William Proxmire of Wisconsin; Professor J. Kenneth Galbraith of Harvard, who was a member of the original advisory committee on oil shale; Professor Morris Garnsey of the University of Colorado, who has given the issue close study; Roscoe Fleming, formerly of the Denver *Post*; Daniel Lynch, regent of the University of Colorado; former Senator John A. Carroll; Joseph Fisher of Resources for the Future; Nelson Poynter, publisher of the St. Petersburg *Times* and of the *Congressional Quarterly*, and others of a similar nature. Such a continuing committee is badly needed to protect the general interest and to shed light on many vexing issues that in the absence of analysis and exposure are likely to be decided wrong. One of its first jobs would be to help defend the government titles to the land, and I hope it would be permitted to act as a "friend of the court" in any important court hearings and trials which may develop. It should also try to protect the mountains from being disfigured by mining and the valleys from being ruined by refuse heaps. Similarly it could insist that the new settlements be modeled on the attractive communities built at Hanford and Oak Ridge by the Atomic Energy Commission and at Norris by the TVA, rather than on the jerry-built mining towns of the past; and in the work and development they could try to find places for the unemployed of the city ghettos to work and live.

Secondly, I would recommend that Congress act now to assign irrevocably the royalties and other incomes from the oil shale lands to investment in the human needs and development of the American people. We have the chance to use the vast future income from these natural resources to build up other natural and human resources in the nation. By spelling out exactly how the revenues from the oil shale could be used to invest in people, we would be able to solicit and obtain the sustained interest of those groups concerned with improving the quality of life in this country. And we could demonstrate to citizens just how their vast patrimony could be used to improve their condition. In this way we should be able to obtain a greater degree of interest from men and women who might otherwise be apathetic.

This was the device we used in trying to save the offshore oil for the nation. It should be even more useful in dealing with the greater resources now embedded in the shale of the upper Colorado basin. This is why I introduced a bill in the Senate in 1965,* following the report of the Oil Shale Advisory Board, that would have assigned this income to a fund under the direction of the Secretary of the Treasury to be used to pay off the national debt. The ultimate income from the oil shale might be much more than enough to pay off the national debt, for even if the public's share did not exceed one-eighth of the sales value of the oil, it could amount ultimately to at least $500 billion if all the oil were recovered.

This bill was intended to illustrate the opportunities available and to make them more explicit. I was well aware that if it became actually possible to pay off the national debt,

* S. 2708, 89th Congress.

many who now lament its size would strenuously resist any attempt to eliminate or reduce it. It has become a good investment for many.

On the whole, however, the further development of the natural and human resources of the nation would probably be more appropriate and productive. At the same time it would arouse more citizen interest. But there is no necessary contradiction between these two sets of purposes. Both could be employed.

Most political scientists have a prejudice against earmarked funds, and insist on separating the revenue and expenditure functions of government. From the purist point of view they are probably right, but they do not take into account the need to arouse the concern and participation of citizens in protecting the public interest or the fact that there are great unmet human needs which our society must try to fulfill in the immediate future but for which it is commonly unwilling to appropriate funds.

I believe it would be wise, for the reasons I have stated to earmark the oil shale income for purposes of human bett ment and for the reduction of the national debt. We are b in need of new housing. There are probably at least 6 million existing units that need to be replaced and ad millions that need to be built at the rate of 2 or 2¹⁄ units a year, of which 500,000 should be for low- and income families. Our schools in the low-income di need additional revenues. The health of the com be safeguarded. We need much more recreatio around our cities as well as additional areas and woods and along the rivers, the seas, this will take money, much money. The oil a source of the funds needed to make our They can help, in time, to make aspirat

. . .

If the predators can be repulsed and if we can retain the shale lands in public ownership, it will be necessary to make some fundamental decisions on how further research and development work is to be carried out and under what terms the oil and minerals are to be produced.

Proposals in 1967 by the Interior Department

In May of 1967, Secretary Udall proposed a set of tentative recommendations that he believed should guide the development of the oil shale resources. He proposed that there be two periods, one for research and the development of the processes, which was not to exceed ten years, and then a second period covering production and the leasing of the oil lands. The Secretary proposed that, if needed, 30,000 acres of oil shale lands be furnished, by exchange or other methods, to the company or group licensed for research and development. Since the present law limits each company to 5,180 acres, this provision clearly looked in the direction of the present consortium which is conducting the work at Anvil Points. For while this is headed by Mobil Oil, it includes six separate companies, which qualify for the total lease of the 30,000 acres.

Since it would undoubtedly be the richest lands that would be leased, the amounts involved would be tremendous. It is reliably estimated that about 100 billion barrels of oil are contained in the 30,000 acres adjacent or close to the Rifle plant. Enormous sums would therefore be involved in such an exchange.

The Secretary proposed that payment to the government or the right to extract oil should be on a sliding-scale basis, depending on the rate of "net profit" on investment made by the producer, instead of a flat percentage of the unit price. There would be a minimum royalty of 3 percent of the sales

value of the product, then on "net profits" in excess of this amount but less than 10 percent, the government's share would be 10 percent of this figure. If the net profits exceeded 10 percent but were less than 20 percent, the government would get 30 of this excess. Finally, on all profits over 20 percent the government's share was to be one-half. On the basis of the experience with offshore oil, it was estimated that this would be equal to 16½ percent of gross sales price and 30 percent of profits. This indicates that profits were expected to be 50 percent of gross price.

The theory behind this proposal was that if the project was relatively unsuccessful, the developer was not to be burdened with the heavy fixed charge on each barrel of oil sold, but that if the venture should prove highly profitable, the government as owner was entitled to a liberal share in the gains. This was to increase as the profits increased.

This seemed on the whole to be a just arrangement, but there were at least two difficulties connected with it. The first was that the Treasury definition of "net profits" was taken after the 27½ percent depletion allowance had been deducted dollar for dollar from what were ordinarily considered to be "net profits." Deducted also were the over-liberal allowances for drilling and development costs. The consequence of all this was that the "net profits" shown by the Treasury statistics were in general only about half what they would amount to in the case of the nonextractive industries. In some cases, these deductions resulted in no net taxable profits being shown. This "loophole" certainly needs to be closed in any final agreement that may be made.

A second danger was that the oil companies might be able to charge off, as an operating expense, costs from other operations of the companies. Since these companies will be engaged in many other activities in which the government does not receive any portion of the net profits, there would naturally be a temptation for them to shift a considerable portion of over-head and managerial costs to the shale oil activities, since by doing so the amounts paid to the government will be reduced.

The oil companies are opposed to the sliding-scale profit-sharing proposals of the Secretary. They wanted to substitute the more usual royalty payment of a fixed percentage of sales price per barrel. However, instead of the usual 12½ percent (i.e., one-eighth) now paid on the oil from land drillings, or the one-sixteenth on oil from the continental shelf, the oil companies asked that the royalty should only be 5 percent (one-twentieth) of the sales price. They in-sisted that the lower rate was necessary because of the high risks involved in the whole process.

This dispute shows the necessity for knowing the actual cost figures at the Anvil Points plant. These figures must be available to the Department of the Interior and it would be a public service if a congressional committee were to subpoena the records and make them public. This would certainly help in forming a more intelligent judgment of what the terms should be for leasing the oil and mineral rights.

A second major point of dispute between Interior and the private oil companies is that of patents. Secretary Udall wants to have these pooled and made freely available to all users. This is opposed by the companies, who want the right of exclusive use of patents. They stress the work already done and the future work that will be done by the corpora-tions themselves. Interior emphasizes that its proposal calls for the public to be a junior or sleeping partner in this project because of its ownership of the resource and hence interested in both the possible inventions and the processes that may be developed.

It will be remembered that the federal government spent some $15 million on experimental and developmental work at Anvil Points by 1954. Much of the plant continues to be used by the consortium headed by Mobil Oil, while the basic gas-combustion process now used in the retorting phase was originated and developed by the Bureau of Mines.

Furthermore, if nuclear energy is used in the *in situ* processes, the co-operation of the Atomic Energy Commission and the utilization of the methods developed by them will be essential. Billions of public dollars have been spent and more will have to be spent for this purpose. At the very least there should be the widest competitive use of this process. And while Standard Oil of Indiana has taken out a specific patent for using nuclear power to fracture oil shale, this has necessarily been built upon the prior efforts of the government.

There is a third impending source of conflict between the government and any private producers who may qualify for exploiting the resource. This is the proper care of the residue left over from the production process. If the *in situ* method is used, especially with the use of nuclear energy, the surface of the area will be left substantially as it is now; the glorious valleys will remain largely undisturbed and the problem will be of minimum proportions. But if the mining and crushing method has to be used, the problem will be huge and pressing. For economical operation, a plant will have to have an enormous intake of shale rock. Even with oil-rich rock running 30 gallons to the ton, the extracted oil will only amount to about a sixth of the weight—leaving the remaining five-sixths in the form of crushed ash.

The five-sixths remaining will be in loose form and hence will take up more space than the original shale. What is to be done with this? The first tendency of a production man would be merely to dump it outside the plants.

But this would be a catastrophe. The volume would be staggering.—For economical operation, a mining-crushing complex should produce, as we have pointed out, 50,000 barrels of oil a day. To do this with shale running at 30 gallons to the ton, an input of at least 70,000 tons of shale a day or about 25 million tons a year will be needed.

The residue from this, as I have said, would be over 60 thousand tons a day and on a yearly basis over 20 million tons, probably occupying nearly a sixth more space than the original rock. Where the oil content of the shale is less, the residue will be greater.

Since many plants will be built if the shale is developed on any large scale, one shudders at the prospect of the ugliness of the dumps replacing the beauty of the mountains, of the destruction of wildlife from the poisonous acids washed into the streams. Secretary Udall, a sincere conservationist, wants the Interior Department to regulate and control dumping. The oil companies shy away from this prospect since it would increase expense and make some developments unprofitable. They protest that they love scenery as much as anyone and can be trusted to protect it. The best possible solution would be for the crushed shale after treatment to be replaced in the mines that have been dug. This would require skillful management to prevent interference with current operations, but it is not impossible. It would have the great advantage of not disfiguring the scenery and minimizing the flow of acids and solid matter into the rivers.

Two further issues deal with the taxation of the oil profits and the distribution of the government's royalties. The oil companies will undoubtedly try to have the 27½ percent depletion allowance apply on the oil taken from government-owned land. The theoretical argument for the depletion allowance is that it is designed to compensate the owners for the gradual exhaustion of a limited natural asset wholly owned by private interests. But this has been carried to an absurd and unjust degree when the average rate of taxation of the profits of oil corporations is only half, or less than that, of the normal corporate rate.

In the case of oil drawn from shale owned by the people through their government, the argument is entirely false. It is the government's asset, not the oil companies', that will be depleted, and to compensate private producers who are not owners for this would be close to highway robbery.

It is therefore crucial that the terms of any contract between the government and private producers be so carefully drawn that the government would still retain title to the shale and other minerals within the earth, and merely license their use. If the Treasury is alert in watching this situation, it should be possible to check the efforts of the oil companies to extend the false principle of the depletion allowance into even more unjustifiable fields.

It is indeed possible that the desire of the companies to fasten down their claim to the depletion allowance, as well as to avoid royalty and lease payments, may be behind the efforts to transfer the oil shale from the public to the private operators.

Finally, at some stage the Congress and the people should consider whether the present arrangements for the division of any royalties or lease payments are fair and just. The Mineral Leasing Act, which now governs this matter, provides that $52\frac{1}{2}$ percent of the receipts go to the federal reclamation states and be used for further reclamation work. These are the eighteen states lying west of the Missouri River and east of the Sierras, an area of low rainfall. Then $37\frac{1}{2}$ percent of the receipts would go to the state where the mineral is mined, to be used for the purposes of education; this, unlike the reclamation portion, would be confined to Colorado, Utah and Wyoming. Under present laws, only the remaining 10 percent would go to the federal government.

The claims of the low-rainfall and mountain states can be understood and appreciated. The minerals lie within their borders, and it is natural for them to ask why they should not be the ones to profit from their use. But we should never forget that the oil shale land belongs to the federal government and not to the states. It was acquired from the Mexican government as a result of a war in which soldiers from all parts of the country served. Since the lands west of the Missouri were virtually unsettled at the time, very few soldiers were from this territory. The war may have been unjust, but it was primarily fought by soldiers from east of the Missouri, and the conscience or "face-saving" money paid to Mexico for the lands came from the Treasury of the United States and hence from the people of the nation.

Furthermore, there are few lands left where further reclamation would be economical. Most of the available water is already pledged to specific projects and irrigation has been carried up into high altitudes where the growing season is short and the yields relatively scanty. I can think of few purposes needing the vast income that may accrue from oil shale less than does reclamation.

While the children and young people of these states undoubtedly could profit from having more money spent for education, their needs are no greater than those of most other states. They are in fact distinctly less than those of the children of the Southern and Southwestern states and in the ghettos of our great cities.

There is a final consideration. The development of the oil shale industry will have been made possible by experimental work carried on at federal expense. This is true even of the conventional mining-crushing-retorting process, for the national government's initial expenditure of $15 million in the decade 1944–1954 laid the basis for later development. If the *in situ* method is used along with nuclear energy, then the federal government will be responsible for virtually the entire development. It has been the American people who have paid out the tens of billions of dollars required. It would be only proper for the federal government to recoup the enormous expenditures it has incurred.

The danger in raising the issue of how the receipts should be shared is of course that it may divide those who might otherwise be united in defending the rights of the general public vis-à-vis the oil companies. The eighteen reclamation states are, moreover, a powerful political force. While their populations, with the exception of California and Texas, are relatively small and their representation in the House limited, they are a large and indeed a dominant force in the Senate. Whether Republicans or Democrats, they generally move together in the common interests of their region. They tend to favor private developers as against the general public, since they believe this will build up their states more quickly. This gives material benefit to merchants and manufacturers, and in the process increases land values.

The weakness in the ranks of the public would be intensified by a bitter struggle over the division of receipts. The oil companies would take full advantage of the cleavage. It would seem desirable, therefore, to work out some compromise that would give a smaller but substantial share to both the reclamation and the oil shale states, to be used for general purposes.

Secretary Udall's proposal is largely based on the assumption that there will ultimately be a competitive oil shale industry. This will probably be more possible with the *in situ* method than with the mining-crushing method, since the latter requires a much larger investment of fixed capital.

Professor Morris E. Garnsey of the University of Colorado is very skeptical as to whether the companies will in fact compete, and doubts that there will be genuine competitive bidding for extraction rights once the research and development period is over. Therefore, he urges that the work be assigned either to a government agency such as the TVA or to a mixed public-private body modeled upon the Communications Satellite Corporation. This is a possibility, and perhaps is desirable, especially if the private companies refuse to act,, but there will have to be a much greater increase in public awareness before it can become a political reality.

Later Developments

While this chapter was passing through the press, the prospects for the public took a turn for the better. Previously, as stated, Solicitor Barry had refused to make a mass attack on the Zweifel claims and had insisted that they must instead be taken up one by one. In testimony before the Senate Interior Committee, and in private conversations with Interior officials, I protested against this attitude and pointed out that since there were many thousands of claims, such a policy would mean that the overwhelming majority would not be challenged and might in time acquire validity.

In spite of what I believed was the good faith of Secretary Udall, the legal branch of the Interior Department continued to refuse publicly to move on any large scale. Solicitor Barry, however, resigned in the late spring of 1968 and shortly thereafter the Department issued a ruling which opened the way to a possible change of policy.* This correctly declared that dawsonite came under the Mineral Leasing Act of 1920 as a sodium compound and not under the Mining Law of 1872 as alumina. If this ruling is upheld, it would mean that the title to the public lands concerned could not be alienated but that the right to extract the dawsonite could be given by Interior under a mutual agreement as to the terms of compensation to be paid to the government.

While the ruling applied only to some cases where there

* In justice to Solicitor Barry it should be recorded that the very able brief in the Shell Oil case was apparently prepared under his direction although not issued until after he left the Department. He also made the persuasive argument in the Coleman case before the Supreme Court, which opened up the May decisions of the Court of Appeals in the Tenth Circuit in the Snyder and Garula cases.

was a direct conflict between pre-1920 mining claims and the 1965–66 leasing claims, the decision created a precedent which *if followed up* could be used to overthrow the Zweifel and other 1965–66 claims. For the dawsonite claims, it will be remembered, were made under the 1872 Mining Law.

The second set of developments were decisions by the Supreme Court and the Tenth Circuit. In the Coleman case, the Supreme Court ruled unanimously * that claims could be denied if the mineral was not marketable, while the Circuit Court held † that the Secretary could refuse to patent a claim if no genuine discovery had been made. These may have a collateral influence on the final fate of two previous District Court decisions. Then on August 6 the Bureau of Land Management, reversed the previous policy of the Solicitor's office and began action to invalidate 400,000 acres of the Zweifel claims in Rio Blanco, Garfield and Moffat counties. But it would be foolish to claim final victory. It will take time and determination to dislodge Zweifel from his long head start. Those decisions in 1966 and 1967 had seemingly prohibited the Interior Department from declaring pre-1920 claims as invalid because of a failure to develop them. The decisions by the District Court were, in turn, seemingly in harmony with and were based upon an extraordinary unanimous decision of the U.S. Supreme Court in the Virginia-Colorado case ‡ which had held that the Interior Department could not finally cancel such claims because of any failure to perform the so-called assessment work, even if after such cancellation no appeals had been taken for years by the aggrieved parties.

That decision by the Supreme Court had always seemed to many of us to have been poor law and bad public policy. The subsequent decisions by the District Court brought the whole

* *U.S. v. Coleman* 20 L.Ed. 170.
† U.S. Court of Appeals, Tenth Circuit, May 1968. *Udall v. Snyder; Udall v. Garula.*
‡ *Ickes v. Virginia-Colorado Development Co.* 295 U.S. 639 (1935).

issue of the pre-1920 claims to fever heat. For such claims were being bought up on a wide scale by speculators and by oil companies, although it was 40 years or more since they had been filed. During that time no developmental work had been done. It had certainly been the intention of Congress in 1920 to outlaw the future transfer of oil shale lands to private ownership and to substitute for this the government retention of the title with leasing rights to individuals subject to terms mutually agreed upon between government and claimants. It was therefore stretching the "grandfather" clause of the 1920 Act not only to the very limit but even beyond it to grant title to private claimants who had failed to perform some of the vital requirements of the 1872 Mining Law.

The public interest seemed to be in mortal danger in 1967 because the Circuit Court was bound to be influenced from above by the Virginia-Colorado decision and from below by the two District Court decisions. In my conversations with the Secretary and other officials of Interior I therefore urged that the case for the government should be argued on appeal by the ablest of the government attorneys.

These cases * were argued on appeal before the Circuit Court in early August. No one can prophesy where judicial logic may lead but it would seem hard for the Court to turn its back on its two recent decisions. What the Supreme Court will do is an interesting question: Will it follow its recent lead in the Coleman case or revert to Virginia-Colorado?

A third favorable development was the issuance by the Interior Department in late May of an unsigned bulletin entitled *Prospects for Oil Shale Development, Colorado, Utah, Wyoming*. In the concluding pages of this report, the terms of the previous 1967 memorandum on leasing and development were in effect superseded. Since there were ample oil shale deposits in private hands and since the companies already had knowledge of existing technology from the experimental work

* *Oil Shale Corporation v. Udall; Snyder v. Udall.*

at Rifle and by Tosco and Union, the Department observed *
"it would be most appropriate that industry undertake the first
ventures." Following this, the Department stated that "a second
plant could be constructed which would permit production of
shale oil at more economically attractive levels."

If this challenge were not accepted by private industry the
Department demurely stated,† "the question will arise as to
the appropriate Federal policy and action in the development
of the oil shale resource. In that event the Federal Government
should seek to determine the reasons for industry inaction and
reassess all aspects of Federal policy."

Looking forward to the leasing of the right to mine and
extract oil from the shale, the Department favored two sets of
leases, one for the thin surface formations and the other for
the thick deep seams. These were to be let on the basis of
competitive bids, with a minimum price set by the Department
and to be paid for by a combination of bonus and royalties
with payments delayed until production was under way.

Finally, in late May of 1968, the Department submitted an
extraordinary brief of over 1,250 pages in the Winegar (Shell
Oil) and D. A. Shale cases. Here it argued with a wealth of
evidence that the pre-1920 claimants had not made any valid
"discovery" of the shale which they claimed. If the Department
continues to stand by the contentions of this brief, it will be
hard for the pre-1920 claimants to win their cases. For in addition nearly all the claimants slept on their alleged "rights." I
believe the legal doctrine of "laches" still applies.

On the whole the Department's present position is far more
hopeful than it was a year ago. But the results still hang in
the balance and if the political climate should shift, we may
still have private interests assuming the ownership of these
resources or obtaining their use without adequate payment
being made to the public.

---

* *Prospects for Oil Shale Development,* p. 77.
† *Ibid.,* p. 78.

3

Some Ethical Problems of Politicians

The recent case of Congressman Adam Clayton Powell together with other incidents has raised anew profound questions of political and congressional ethics. There is, once again, an uneasy feeling among the public that legislators are corrupt, that our democratic processes are tainted with fraud and that the whole political structure of our country is decadent.

Perhaps a politician who has been retired from office after nearly a quarter of a century in the politics of Chicago and in the Senate of the United States may be competent to address himself to that subject.

. . .

Let me start by saying that conditions are not as bad as most people believe and that, contrary to current belief, the level of congressional behavior is relatively high. Congress is today a far more ethical body than it was in the days of Daniel Webster or during the Gilded Age following the Civil War. It is more representative of the people of the nation than was the millionaires' club of Hanna, Aldrich, Platt and Depew when David Graham Phillips wrote his philippic, *The Treason of the Senate,* and Lincoln Steffens published *The Shame of the Cities.*

There are, however, built-in forces now at work that if not corrected will cause our government to be controlled by and for the wealthy rather than all the people, to become a plutocracy rather than a democracy. We are indeed well along on that road.

The immediate hurdle that any aspirant for either the House or the Senate must face is the terrific cost of running for office. Elections today cost enormous sums of money and this requirement is one of the most corrupting influences in public life.

I shall start with a few truths that should be obvious to all, though the public persists in ignoring them. First, we cannot have a democracy without elections nor can we have elections without candidates. Voters must make choices and in a democracy these cannot be made in a vacuum. That is one of the differences between the free world and the one-party states such as Russia and the Communist bloc, where political competition is forbidden. The man or woman who runs for office is therefore performing a civic duty of a high order. If this is done without mudslinging or corruption, the candidate, whether successful or not, deserves the thanks of society.

Second, the performance of this civic duty entails enormous expense. Television and radio are extremely costly; office headquarters and staff must be paid for; travel and hotels are not free; the telephone company is not a charitable organization; printers and billboard companies are not in business for their health; and many voters, because of illness, indifference or family cares, have to be transported to the polls on election day or need baby-sitters to spell them. All of these activities are both necessary and honorable and all of them cost money— lots of money. They are costing more and more with every election.

As an example, in 1966 we found that one twenty-second spot announcement on prime time over Chicago's leading television station cost $1,900. Six seconds of this time had to be used by a station disclaimer so that we only got 14 seconds of net time for the $1,900. How can a poor man play in that league? How can he even get admitted to the ball park?

To put the dilemma in still broader terms, how can a political party that aims primarily to defend the poor, the weak and the disinherited get the money with which to fight campaigns for them? And yet to keep the democratic system of popular choice going, many candidates do make such sacrifices, and when they do so, they run smack up against the existing federal laws and the predominant opinion of the affluent. For I suppose that the majority of the citizens, or at least a large share of them, regard political activity as somewhat discreditable and would think less of themselves if they contributed to the support of a political candidate.

Then to make matters even more difficult, Congress under the pressure of public opinion limited expenditures by a candidate for the House to $5,000, for the Senate to $25,000 and for the Presidency to $3 million. The senatorial limit might be realistic in a small state like Vermont, and then probably only for an incumbent Senator like George Aiken who was well known, respected, and beloved. But try to run for the Senate on $25,000 in California, New York, Pennsylvania, Illinois, Ohio, Texas and Massachusetts and a host of other states!

That would be ludicrous, and anyone who abided by that limit would, in racetrack lingo, be left at the post. In practice, as I shall show later, the actual costs run up into the hundreds of thousands and often into the millions of dollars.

How is this carried out? Structurally it is done by having the friends and managers of a candidate set up a multitude of committees, which are kept organizationally separate from those of either the candidate himself or his party, to receive and pay out added funds. In House and Senate races these committees do not have to report and in the presidential race they can report separately. This device was first developed, I believe, by the friends and supporters of Wendell Willkie in the 1940 campaign. They organized a number of separate committees of which Willkie professed ignorance. Each one of these committees successfully contended that it was independent and that, at most, the limit would apply to each one taken separately but not to the galaxy of Willkie committees as a whole. In this way several times the specified limit was successfully and legally spent. I think every subsequent presidential candidate has been compelled to use similar devices.

This same system has been carried over into Senate and House campaigns. I remember testimony before a senatorial committee about the expenditures by various committees acting primarily in behalf of Senator Robert Taft in the senatorial election of 1950. These, only partially totalled, came to over $1½ million.

Candidates therefore are forced to get friends to organize citizens' committees for them, and in the larger states there will be a host of these, such as business and labor committees, ethnic groups and the like. These often come to a quite bewildering total. The candidate must swear that he doesn't know how much these groups have spent and must disavow responsibility for them. He only swears to expenses made by his own committee, over which he does take responsibility and avow knowledge. Generally, these are for personal expenses, travel and printing.

The more a candidate tries to comply with the spirit as well as with the letter of the law, the less he will know about what his managers are doing. For I repeat, the candidate must swear that he does not know how much was spent for him, or for what purposes, or who contributed how much.

The results are demeaning as well as ineffective. And yet almost no practicing politician dares to confess the truth, lest some of his opponents investigate him, take him up before the law and smear him before an electorate which is ignorant of the facts of life. The average voter still believes, or pretends to believe, that elections do not or should not cost much money. Our grandmothers and great-grandmothers spread the story of babies being brought from the great unknown by storks, who then deposited them under the lilac bushes, but today we have exchanged such ideas for faith in the immaculate election of candidates. Guilty silence perpetuates the myth, which prevents corrective action to clear up some of the real abuses that have grown up in the darkness.

On the basis of my five senatorial campaigns and my wife's two state-wide races, I believe that the high costs of election, combined with an inequitable system of financial aid, is one of the worst influences in guiding the present selection and election of candidates and in the policies and programs they enact once they are in office.

Consider some of the recent revelations: Governor Nelson Rockefeller filed a statement on January 2, 1967, according to the New York *Times,* that he had spent over $5 million in his 1966 campaign for re-election. With this, according to the *National Observer,* he purchased and had produced between 3,000 and 4,000 radio and television programs. These and other expenditures in his behalf were very helpful and probably decisive in reversing the highly unfavorable polls taken during the first part of the year, which were reported at first as being at least 2 to 1 against the Governor, and which have since been admitted to have been 3 to 1. Let me hasten to say that I regard Governor Rockefeller as an excellent chief executive and a highly qualified public figure. But what would have happened had a poor man, or a man from the middle class, of equal merit—but with no access to millions—been faced with a similar situation? In all probability he would have gone down to crushing defeat. Governor Rockefeller's opponent, Frank O'Connor, reported expenditures of only $576,000.

In Pennsylvania a relatively unknown businessman spent at least $1.4 million to win the Democratic primaries, only to lose in the general election after spending an almost equal sum. In the New York City mayoral election of 1965, John Lindsay spent $2.4 million and his opponent, Abe Beame, $2.3 million in the primary and general election. In California in 1964, one Democratic candidate for U.S. Senator is reliably reported to have spent $1 million in the primary and his opponent is said to have spent $628,000. It is estimated that the total primary expenditures of both parties in the senatorial primary were around $3.6 million, and if the general election is included, the senatorial candidates spent at least $5 million.

No one knows how much money was spent in the 1962 race for the Senate in Massachusetts, or in the 1964 Senatorial contest in New York. Murray Levin in his study of the former campaign seems to imply that well over a million dollars were spent by the Massachusetts contestants, while in New York each side probably spent in the millions.

In the senatorial election of 1966 in the relatively small state of Oregon, Governor Hatfield reported expenditures of $528,000, and his opponent, Robert Duncan, $277,000. A congressman from New York stated that in 1964 he spent $194,000 to get elected. High costs are even characteristic of running for seats in most state legislatures. I found them high thirty years ago when I ran in my ward for a seat on the Chicago Board of Aldermen.

Most of the figures given represent only the expenses that were reported; generally the real expenditures are vastly more. Since the 1966 election, I have found that the total expenditures for my none-too-frequent radio and television programs, newspaper advertising, billboards, etc. came to between $350,000 and $400,000.

It is obvious that modern campaigns have become so frightfully costly that the attempt to put unrealistic ceilings on campaign expenses has proved completely ineffective.

It has become increasingly impossible for a poor man to run for public office, and a man of moderate means can do so only if he has the backing of people with great wealth. With the rapid shrinkage of independent enterprise through the merger process, economic life is also becoming more tightly controlled by a relatively small group. This increases the candidates' dependence on financial backing.

Hanging over the head of every candidate, moreover, is the prospect of a substantial deficit. A candidate may have insulated himself from his committees as I did whenever I ran, but if the books do not balance, he is held morally responsible for the deficit. He cannot run out on the creditors even though he was ignorant of the expenditures.

If he is victorious, this may not be too much of a problem. Victors generally find friends, though not always at once. Even so, it would generally take me close to a full six years to meet the deficits of the past campaign, and I would generally get my head above water only in time to start the next race. But for the defeated candidate the deficit can be a crushing burden. All but stalwart friends tend to fall away from a loser. In homely language, politicians describe this situation by saying that there is nothing more lonely than last year's bird's nest.

I have known candidates who, having mortgaged their homes and borrowed on their life insurance policies, found themselves losers and were prostrated by their heavy campaign debts. Such examples discourage good men from running and handicap the party of the lower income groups.

The people ultimately pay many times over for these campaign costs, but this comes after the election in covert, anti-social ways, such as special interest legislation and ill-considered appointments. It would be far better for the people to pay before the election and to do so openly. This would save money, reduce corruption and permit able and good men of meager means to run for office.

By drifting and refusing to act, we will inevitably find ourselves ruled by a plutocracy or government by the rich instead of a democracy. Indeed, we may have already arrived at such a state. I have no prejudice against the rich as such. I agree with Gilbert and Sullivan that

> "Hearts just as pure and fair
> May beat in Belgrave Square
> As in the lowly air
> Of Seven Dials."

I am therefore glad that the former prejudice against men of wealth running for office has been broken, and I agree that it is an asset to have members of the Rockefeller and Kennedy families in public life.

But I do not want, and I believe the American people do not want, our officials to be confined to the rich or to those whom the rich can control by their donations. We should make it possible for able and good men of moderate means— or no means at all—to run for public office with a greater prospect of success. Otherwise we will close off public life to people and interests who need to feel that they are a part of society and can make contributions to it.

Moreover, excellent as specific individuals may be, a Congress or an executive branch largely composed of men of great wealth and their protégés will inevitably become a class-dominated legislature in which the crucial decisions will serve the interests of the affluent. But the poor and the less affluent are not only people with equal rights; they also comprise the majority of the population and, if we take $10,000 for a family of four as the dividing line, they are a full four-fifths of the nation.

Although there are many exceptions, of whom the late Senator Lehman was the most notable example during my period in the Senate, men usually follow their own interests or those of their class. This is what they know and believe to be right. We therefore do not get the balance of interests necessary for a sound and enduring democracy.

The great need is for campaigns to be so democratically financed that candidates and parties will not be under obligation to large contributors. Only under these conditions can citizens and parties of modest means compete on equitable terms.

Probably the ideal solution would be for large numbers of people voluntarily to make relatively small contributions so that campaigns would be adequately financed without the parties and candidates incurring excessive obligations to any individual or interest. The difficulty is to persuade enough people to take sufficient interest and to do this in time. The quarter of the population in poverty or its fringes is, however, completely unable to give. Another quarter, in the lower economic middle class, has such pressing personal and family needs and desires that they really cannot afford to contribute to political campaigns, and it is an almost heroic act when they do. Many of the middle and upper layers of the middle class are indifferent about giving to candidates and parties, and this is true of many of the affluent as well. Others wake up to the issues too late to be of much help. But modern campaigns are like wars. They cannot be fought or financed by guerrilla bands of amateurs; they need preparation and advance planning and financing.

It would be excellent if parties could be supported by dues-paying members, and the Minnesota Democratic–Farmer Labor Party has made heroic efforts in this direction in an effort to meet running expenses in the periods between campaigns. But past efforts to finance campaigns by small contributions have been relatively unsuccessful. The most effective device thus far has been the political dinner. Although there have been some abuses in this field, it is on the whole the least objectionable way of raising large sums of money. It does distribute the costs and partially frees candidates and parties from excessive dependence upon a few. By giving to the participants a mixture of information, education, entertainment, participation and fellowship, it can be and commonly is an excellent and ethical way of raising money. It would be tragic if, out of false prejudice created by the Dodd and Dulski cases, people discarded this useful method. But even with the dinners, the costs of campaigning—notably for television—have increased so much more rapidly than receipts that the problem of campaign financing has grown rather than diminished.

When I was chairman of the first Senate Committee on Ethics in 1950–51, I became convinced that the most effective way to cope with these problems was for the government to do what Theodore Roosevelt had advocated a long time ago: finance the major share of campaign costs. Since then my former colleagues Richard and Maurine Neuberger not only agreed but introduced bills to effect it. The Commonwealth of Puerto Rico has adopted such a system, which seems to have worked well, and Japan has a somewhat modified program of aid. During 1967, both Senator Russell Long and the Administration advanced proposals for such public financing. Senator Long's bill was adopted as a matter of "principle" by Congress, although its full implementation has been postponed.

I can think of nothing more necessary than such legislation, and while any measure will have some weaknesses, the preponderance of benefit is on the side of each and all of these bills.

I believe that from a composite of these bills and from further suggestions made by Senators Lee Metcalf and Albert Gore, a very excellent final measure could be prepared without excessive difficulty. I would like to mention some of the desirable features which in my judgment should be included.

First, the Long and Metcalf bills in their final forms overcame certain crucial weaknesses in previous proposals for government financing: (1) they involved the participation of the individual voter in the financing process, and (2) they made funds available during a campaign and not merely afterward.

Looking back, I see that my earlier proposals for the outright government financing of election costs were subject to the just criticism that they did not involve the individual voters. The government was to pay out the money at the rate of approximately ten cents a registered voter to candidates who were on the ballot for President, Senator or Representative. Individual contributions of money were to be barred, but those of time and effort were permitted. Along with many good results, these provisions would, however, have greatly weakened the voters' sense of participation in political matters, which needs to be encouraged rather than weakened. Secondly, money for expenses is needed during the campaign period, not afterward.

Both of these important purposes will be served by giving, by one means or another, certificates or scrip to voters, which they can then endorse personally in favor of a Presidential candidate. In this way the individual voter can take part in the financing. Moreover the voter should be permitted to transfer this voucher to the candidate of his choice or to a committee authorized to act for him. This would permit a more decentralized form of financing than the Administration bills originally permitted. It would not make the party committees all powerful—which was a legitimate criticism of both my plan and that of the Johnson Administration. The certificate might also be turned over by the individual to other bodies, such as the Americans for Constitutional Action, the John Birch Society, or the Americans for Democratic Action, the National Association of Manufacturers or COPE, the political arm of the AFL-CIO, etc., if these were approved by the candidates. The interest of these groups could therefore also be enlisted, and they could help in the collection of funds for candidates. As the Comptroller General (or his agents) received these certificates, he would turn them in for redemption and make payments to those groups. The candidates and parties would therefore receive funds when they were needed and not have to borrow on the expectation of being reimbursed.

Owing to the great increase in campaign costs since 1951, I believe my earlier ceiling of ten cents per registered voter is now altogether too low and that a contribution of one dollar per voter for the Presidency would be reasonable.

In my judgment this system should, as Senator Gore has urged, be applied to Senate and House candidates as well. These, as a matter of fact, are the candidates who need money the most and whose need poses some of the most troublesome problems. If a certificate of one dollar be granted for the Presidency, then I suggest that an equal sum be granted for combined contributions to the appropriate Senate and House candidates. This could either be in the form of a single dollar certificate, which could then be given by the voter to a candidate for one or the other of these offices, or two fifty-cent certificates could be issued—one for the Senate and the other for the House. On the whole I would prefer the latter, since the former method would tend to produce friction between candidates of the same party.

I am aware that neither the dominant parties in one-party states nor their incumbent Senators and Representatives would like to have this system finance their opponents. The minorities in these states are at present often hopelessly handicapped in finances as well as other respects, and the dominant parties would naturally like to keep them so. But this is not good for the country. Every state should have a vigorous opposition party so that issues can be threshed out and parties and candidates kept on their toes. Providing grants for the candidates for the Senate and House would help to build up such a two-party system.

The problem of third parties is a real one. On the whole the two-party system has served us well. It has permitted us to adapt our institutions to changing conditions and to do so without endangering the fundamental unity of the nation. It seems to be a far better system than that of multiple parties which prevailed in France under the Third and Fourth Republics. But at times the two parties may become so much alike in aims and methods as to deny the voters any significant choice. This was roughly the situation between the Republican and Democratic Parties between 1890 and 1896, and again in 1904, and possibly from 1922 to 1930 as well. Under these conditions a third party may be not only desirable but inevitable. Any system of financing should not close off this possibility. The mere threat of a third party will help to keep the two major parties from becoming virtually identical.

There are two ways of achieving this. The first would be

to permit the assignment of the certificates to candidates or parties that in any given state were on the ballot. The second would be to require that a party or its candidates could cash its certificates only if its candidates had polled a certain percentage of the votes—say 5 to 10 percent—in the preceding election in that state. This would not be too much of a handicap; for if a minority party does represent a substantial body of opinion, it could earlier poll the small qualifying percentage of votes without a public subvention. It is the 10 percent or so of "swing" voters who now decide elections and who have to be wooed in an expensive manner by radio, television and other advertisements. The true believers do not need such enticements, and if they represent any considerable body of public opinion they will generally be able to get on the ballot without such initial aid.

Whether public financing should be extended to the primaries or confined to the general election is another question. In states where one party is dominant, the primary is commonly far more important than the election. Obviously the community cannot finance an unlimited number of aspirants, few of them commanding any real popular support. One solution might be to permit the assignment of the House and Senate certificates to be made after the election to those candidates who polled 10 percent or more of the total primary vote for that office. This would reduce some of the financial fears that stop many from running in the primaries. One weakness would be that its use by disappointed supporters of a defeated primary candidate would diminish the final chances of his successful opponents and hence promote party dissension. But this fault seems minor compared with its benefits.

Just as Senators and Representatives from one-party states would not want to provide financing for candidates from the opposite party, neither will those who are well entrenched wish to include the primaries. For these subventions would undoubtedly encourage rivals in both the primaries and the general elections who at present hesitate to take the field. But since incumbents should always be subject to challenge, this would be a healthy innovation. There is the danger however of loading down the bill with enough politically unpopular features to prevent Congress from approving it even for presidential elections.

A few years ago, the President's Committee on Election Financing proposed that we provide tax inducements for private contributions rather than outright public subventions. If no safeguards were to be included in such a law, it would help the wealthy to dominate our political life even more completely than they do now. The public would thus be asked to underwrite in whole or in part the private contributions of the wealthy. Having tried over the years to reduce the erosion of our tax system, I would prefer to have the financing of elections faced directly through the spending process rather than to do so indirectly through a further weakening of the individual and corporate income tax, which would diminish revenues.

Finally, the use of assignable certificates along the lines suggested by Senators Metcalf and Gore would encourage private participation, which is advanced as one of the arguments in support of a tax stimulus plan. But while public financing is desirable as a replacement for private contributions as the main form of financing, it should not completely displace the private givers. These could continue to donate not only their effort but also a limited amount of money. I would fix the upper limit for an individual contribution to any one candidate at $100, with reporting for all contributions over $25. If a further stimulus is desired, then the first $25 could be deducted directly, dollar for dollar, from the amount of taxes that would otherwise be paid. This would be better than merely deducting the contribution from taxable income, since under the latter plan the progressive scale of the income tax would mean that the larger a man's income the more he could shift his contributions onto the government and hence onto other and less affluent taxpayers.

There is one further campaign measure that needs to be adopted. This is for the radio and television stations to provide a certain amount of free time to the more important candidates for national and state office. The chief commercial asset these stations possess is their monopoly control over the airwaves, which has been granted to them without charge by the Congress. In 1965 the radio industry made $81 million and television $448 million before taxes. These enterprises are not only extremely profitable but the amount of fixed capital the operators have invested is relatively small. Since these media are now the most expensive of all the campaign requirements, it would seem proper for broadcasters to provide a certain amount of free time to the qualified candidates of parties polling 10 percent of the vote on the last election. This could be set at two or three hours for the presidential candidates and at least one hour for the House and Senate. Candidates for Governor should also be allotted an hour. This time moreover should not be consigned to the "ghetto" hours when few listen or watch, but to the so-called "prime" hours between 6:30 and 10:30 at night. Shortly before his assassination, Robert Kennedy called attention to the importance of the television charges as an item of campaign expense.

Once the election is over and the successful Senator or Representative has assumed office and begun to draw his annual salary of $30,000, he finds that money problems are still with him. State legislators are often in the same fix. If he is careful, a Representative has to brush off those who

would put him under personal obligation by gifts and entertainment, and he has to face the fact that by holding office
he is committed to a series of expenditures which are virtually
inseparable from his formal duties. Thus, it is imperative that
he make frequent trips back to his district or state to discuss
public and local issues with his constituents and to familiarize
himself with their needs and problems. The confirmed Wash-
ingtonians and those primarily interested in foreign affairs
commonly and contemptuously describe these trips as mere
"fence-mending," unworthy of a public representative. They
are instead the very essence of democracy, because they
enable the voters and their elected representatives to communicate with each other in person to their mutual benefit. He
who seeks truly to represent the people must associate with
them. For only so can he vividly realize their needs and problems. Moreover these face-to-face visits are the minimum price
of survival. The Senator or Representative who neglects them
is likely to be retired fairly quickly, and we have lost many
splendid legislators because of their neglect of this simple
duty.

Yet these trips cost not only time but money. Senators are
allowed transportation for only six trips a year, but I would
make at least twenty-four. I used to go back to Illinois at
least two weekends a month while Congress was in session
and spend an additional 45 to 60 days there each fall after
Congress had adjourned. I would visit nearly every one of
the 102 counties in the state at least once in every two years
and the more important counties once a year and generally
twice. I spent about half of my total time in and around
Chicago, where two-thirds of the population of the state is
concentrated. My yearly expenditures for these purposes outside of Chicago would come to between $3,000 and $4,000
a year. Senator Proxmire, who is probably the most tireless
campaigner in the history of the Senate, has made it a prac-

tice throughout his decade of service to go back to Wisconsin
every weekend and while there to meet with approximately
a thousand people a day. I know of no one else who has so
much endurance and self-discipline, but everyone must have
a large degree of it if he is to last.

In recent years Washington has become a tourist center,
and from March until October hundreds of thousands of
visitors throng the city. Tens of thousands came each year
from Illinois and most of them wanted to see their representatives. Mrs. Douglas and I would give two receptions a week
at which, after a short social period, I would speak briefly
and then invite questions. Scarcely a day passed, moreover,
that I did not entertain a bevy of constituents in the Senate
dining room. All this lessened the estrangement that is so
likely to set in between citizens and a far-off and seemingly
impersonal national government. In short, we tried to per-
sonalize government in Washington as we tried to do back
home. But this too cost money—generally about $2,500 a year.

This is an electronic age. A representative cannot neglect
radio and television if he would communicate with his constituents. My wife and I developed a fortnightly program on
current events and issues, which over fifty radio and nine television stations broadcast on public-service time. We had to
pay for the expense of cutting the tapes, and this came to
around $3,000 a year. It is a pleasure to record that the station
owned by my most severe critic, the Chicago *Tribune,* was
also the most generous in granting its facilities.

There were at least two other major sets of expenses. The
first included miscellaneous items ranging from subscriptions
to a wide variety of Illinois newspapers plus technical and
foreign journals, contributions to Illinois churches and charities, to messages and flowers for funerals, weddings and
christenings. These would run annually from $1,250 to $1,500.

Finally, an officeholder has the welcome duty of contributing to the various levels of party activity from the ward organization at the bottom up through the city, county and state to the national committee at the top. In biennial election years the officeholder, seeing the financial plight of colleagues and fellow party members, should feel obliged when he is not running himself to help their personal campaigns. These contributions in my case never fell below $1,500 a year and in the biennial years would generally be at least $2,000.

Each year our Christmas season was made miserable by the sea of cards that poured in upon us, amounting to well over five thousand. My wife and I would spend days going over them, but soon found that the vast majority came from relative strangers and were sent without any real personal affection or concern. At first, like so many others, we tried to return card for card and to compile elaborate mailing lists. But this stripped our Christmas season of all genuine pleasure in showing interest and affection for relatives and friends. Christmas was being turned instead into a desecrated desert of public relations. I shall never forget one Christmas when we spent virtually the entire day opening hundreds of cards and finding each to be as barren as its predecessor. We then and there resolved to leave the competitive Christmas-card racket and return to sending gifts and remembrances to close friends and relations plus checks to a few especially cherished charities. In this way we saved a couple of thousand dollars a year and many days of work for ourselves and staff. I think all of my colleagues were as burdened as we had been but felt locked in by the competitive pressures of politics.

These necessary although quasi-political expenditures amounted to between $12,000 and $14,000 a year, and I paid for all of this out of my salary. In addition, I also paid for the extra living expenses during the time I spent in Chicago, which came to another $3,000. After paying $5,250 as the federal income tax on my basic salary of $30,000 plus $1,000 of property taxes in Chicago and Washington, another payment of $2,250 towards a retirement annuity and few other payments, I would have left out of my salary each year between $6,000 and $7,000. Had it not been for money I earned by lectures and articles, and a small income from investments and annuities, I would not have been able to support my family. As it was, with only one child, we were able to live on about the same scale as when I had been a college professor in Chicago. This was completely satisfactory to us, but I have often wondered what would have happened had I not been able to earn additional money by lecturing and writing—or if, like Senator Dodd, I had had six children to support and educate.

I do not know the answer to these problems of quasi-political expenses. The wealthy can take them in stride. Many get along as we did, but some definitely cannot. I submit that these politicians should not be severely blamed if they accept modest contributions from testimonial dinners, provided only that the donors know for what purpose their money is to be used and that they represent a wide range of the electorate, so that no one person or group will acquire undue influence.

I do not, however, believe the answer is an additional increase in congressional salaries. This would only lead to a further increase in the costs of holding office.

A member of Congress should be aware of two further dangers that will beset him. He should not accept gifts and entertainment that put him under obligation to anyone desiring public favors, or allow his sources of income to involve him in any real conflict of interest with his official duties.

When I won my first Senate election in 1948, I was inundated with presents of liquor, silk, clothes, proffered vacations and even books on art. The names of the donors who suddenly discovered their friendship for me were virtually unknown to me. I decided therefore that they were not friends but rather investors who hoped to put me under obligation so that they might receive future favors. So my wife and I tied up these parcels and sent them back to the givers by express —collect! I thought this would discourage future gifts, but when I arrived in Washington I went through the same experience. The result was that I began to spend an inordinate amount of time deciding which gifts I should refuse and which I could safely accept. Finally I concluded that I should draw a specific line, and I put it at $2.50.

Any such arbitrary limit is of course ludicrous. Some critics have said that I could apparently resist a temptation of $2.49 but feared I would succumb if it cost $2.51. Those who have read Henri Bergson's little book called *Laughter* will remember that he traces the source of laughter to our sense of the absurdity of trying to run life by purely mechanical standards. Something like this was evoked by the collector of internal revenue in Richmond, who testified that at income tax time he generally received a large number of Virginia hams, some of which he would accept and some refuse. When asked where he drew the line, he replied that he usually drew it "at twelve pounds." If the ham weighed less he would accept it, if more, he would return it. My standard may have been equally laughable.

But it saved me time, which I could devote to more important matters, and it kept me from the more open forms of trouble. I said that it proved you could not corrupt a Senator for less than $2.50! And I did not raise the limit in spite of the increase in prices after 1949.

It is also wise to decline offers of paid vacations in Florida, New York or other points. The Kennedy Administration had such rules for all its officials, and these have been continued by President Johnson. There is no reason why Congress should not adopt them for itself.

. . .

A final ethical morass is that of a conflict of interest. Congress insists that Administration officers should not become involved in such conflicts. It is lax, however, in applying such standards to itself. Once I faced such a case when I was offered a large check for speaking before a trade association on behalf of a bill favored by both the association and myself. Fearing that perhaps the fee could be construed as being given to cement my loyalty to the measure, I returned the money and adopted a rule that I would never accept a fee, for speaking or for writing an article, from a group that was working for some piece of legislation or government policy. Of course, I have spoken before such groups without pay, and I have felt that the resulting relationship is much healthier for all sides.

Another subtle form of temptation comes to the lawyers in Congress who are offered retainers by economic interests affected by proposed legislation. This is in the tradition of Webster, who not only accepted such retainers but actually solicited them. The practice is a subterranean form of corruption, and it may extend to many among the Senators, two-thirds of whom are lawyers. In my judgment it would be well if Congress closed the door to this type of conflict of interest. Another abuse is for a legislator to get a commission from law firms for cases referred to them. The potential evils of this practice are obvious.

There remains the question of investments. In the case of family businesses, it is difficult for a man to disentangle himself, but wherever such a conflict exists, it should be revealed. Many years ago during a debate on the basing point system in which I opposed the policies of the steel industry, the thought crossed my mind that my stand might lower the price of U.S. Steel shares, of which I owned a few. I kept on with the fight but immediately sold my shares and invested the proceeds in a mutual investment trust, the holdings of which were so widely distributed as to be unaffected by any legislative action. These and government bonds constituted our sole source of investment during my time in the Senate.

The best way of dealing with most of these subtle temptations is through public disclosure. I first practiced this as an alderman in Chicago from 1939 on, and when I was chairman of the first Senate Committee on Ethics, I recommended it. As a Senator, I continued in this course. In my annual report, I would list the property holdings of both Mrs. Douglas and myself, our income by sources, and the main groups of quasi-official expenses that we had paid out. Then we made our income tax returns and accounts available for inspection by those who wanted to check them.

I believe Congress should require this of all its members. While it may violate one's desire for privacy, it is the best way of protecting congressional honor. Many flagrant cases have weakened public faith in legislative bodies, and that helps to destroy one of the major foundations of democracy itself. Since it is a great honor to serve in Congress, men should be willing to sacrifice some of the privileges that private citizens enjoy.

Disclosure would have many advantages, especially as a deterrent to unethical conduct. Most men go wrong because they think they can do shady things in secret and not be detected. They think they can beat the game and disregard Emerson's advice that "If you would not be known to do a thing, don't do it."

Further, the measure would be self-policing. There would be no indictments, court trials or criminal penalties (except for willful deception in the reporting). The facts would merely be made available for the public to judge. Most men, and especially politicians, desire the good opinion of their fellow citizens, and this remedy, both flexible and self-enforcing, would be persuasive. Not only would disclosure have a good effect on the behavior of members of Congress; it would also be very reassuring to the general public.

I believe the general standards of congressional behavior are relatively high. Under the disclosure provisions, they would become still higher, and Congress would recover the trust and faith it should have as the purified instrument of a people's will. We would gain a spiritual reinforcement in our struggle with the police states for the loyalties of men. And in the meantime, perhaps the members of the public should be more understanding about the financial difficulties of those who are trying to make democracy work and perhaps make them more careful of their own conduct. Both House and Senate with much reluctance are slowly feeling their way towards such a requirement. But they need to move much faster. One more set of scandals may bring the reform about but it would be a dear price that democracy will have to pay for the delay.

4   *Truth in Lending*

Very few people realize that the total personal debt in the United States is almost as great as our national public debt, yet this is the sober truth. In July 1968, the public debt amounted to about $370 billion. The total personal debt in May came to $337 billion, or only $33 billion and 9 percent less. Moreover, while personal debt had doubled during the last 10 years, having increased by $170 billion, the public debt, despite the heavy costs of the Vietnamese war, had risen only by about half as much in dollar terms and less than that relatively. Barring continued war, all signs point to the coming of the time when, despite federal deficits, the personal debt will overtake and exceed the national debt.

There are, of course, two major types of personal debt: mortgages outstanding against non-farm and one- to four-family homes, and consumer credit. The first amounted to $237 billion in March 1967, and the latter totaled $100 billion in May 1968. Consumer credit, in turn, was made up of $79 billion of installment credit and $21 billion of non-installment credit. Automobile credit was the major form of installment debt and amounted to between $32 and $33 billion. The installment debt for other forms of consumer goods, chiefly, but not exclusively, for durable items such as radio and television sets, washing machines, furniture and the like, came to approximately $24 billion. Personal loans repayable on the installment plan amounted to a little less than this figure, or $22 billion. Non-installment debt divided between single payment loans, charge accounts and service credit also came to about $21 billion.

When consumer credit was in its infancy a third of a century ago, I was made a public member of the code authority set up by the National Recovery Administration for the consumer finance industry. I tried to take my supposed responsibilities seriously and to become acquainted with some of the salient conditions that we were supposed to regulate. My friend Dr. William T. Foster had been working on this issue for years, and I had learned a great deal from him. Two weaknesses in the industry immediately stood out. The first was that on loans that were gradually repaid in monthly installments the interest was computed not on the declining balance actually owed by the borrower, but instead on the original amount borrowed. This required the borrower to pay interest on amounts that he had already repaid and meant that the real rate of interest was approximately double the one quoted.

I was also struck by the fact that in making loans the personal finance companies would quote their interest rates in monthly rather than yearly terms. At that time, the predominant rate on these loans was $3\frac{1}{2}$ percent a month. They were referred to as "$3\frac{1}{2}$ percent loans," and the fact that they came to 42 percent a year was never mentioned.

At the first meeting of the code authority in 1934, I brought up these facts and suggested that the members of the industry should quote their rates on an annual rather than a monthly basis and charge interest only on the unpaid balance. Never did the temperature of a meeting drop so sharply and so far. A chilling silence set in and the authority shortly adjourned. A few days later, I received a letter suggesting that I might want to resign. I had already resolved to go back to Chicago and resume my teaching duties, and I had many other cares on my mind. So, rather than provoke another struggle, I sent in my resignation. It was one of the few times in my life that I have backed away from a fight and I must confess that over the years I had twinges of conscience over my action.

Fifteen years later, to my great surprise and that of most other people, I found myself a member of the United States Senate. For a full decade I busied myself with other matters such as housing, welfare legislation and the tax structure. But as I watched consumer and personal credit grow like Jack's beanstalk, and as I realized that the old abuses had not been cured, I felt increasingly that I must make amends for my quarter-century of negligence.

I therefore consulted with Milton Semer, a staff expert assigned to the liberal Democratic members of the Banking and Currency Committee of which I was a member. We worked through the fall of 1959 and early in 1960 I introduced the first truth-in-lending bill. It was based on the very simple principle I had tried to develop before on the Consumers' Advisory Board and within the code authority, that the consumer was entitled to know the truth about the credit he used and that the true interest rates should be quoted in annual terms on the outstanding unpaid balance of his debt or the amounts he actually owed.

If my 1934 proposal had caused a chilling silence, my 1960 bill called forth heated denunciation. I had expected opposition from the auto dealers, the finance companies and possibly from the banks. But I was not prepared for the deluge that descended upon us. Not only did these groups and their trade associations line up against us but also the merchants and mail order houses. Into their wake moved the National Association of Manufacturers, the U.S. Chamber of Commerce, the American Bankers Association and the American Bar Association. Then virtually all of the Republicans, with the exception of Senator Case of New Jersey, lined up in opposition and most of the Southern Democrats, including Senator A. Willis Robertson, the chairman of the Banking and Currency Committee. Senator Robertson was especially bitter in his opposition, and I knew we were in for a hard struggle. Year after year I held hearings on the bill before the subcommittee on economic stabilization, of which I was chairman. We would develop a great deal of valuable testimony and then the subcommittee would refuse to report the bill out. Finally, for just one day we got the bill out of the parliamentary sub-cellar, only to have the full committee promptly send it back.

I was continually urged either to give up the struggle or sacrifice the vital sections of the bill. In Illinois I was being laughed at for not being able to pass the bill, while the conservative columnists in Washington were enjoying a field day by calling me an "ineffectual knee-jerk liberal." But I could not bring myself to give up, or to accept a face-saving compromise. For during all this time the importance of consumer credit was rapidly increasing and our hearings were revealing great abuses. The public finally began to awaken from its long slumber of ignorance and indifference. Support came from the credit unions, which then had on their rolls as many as eighteen million members. They were grappling with these very problems in a most constructive way. Under their rules, no local union could charge more than 1 percent a month or 12 percent a year and all interest had to be computed on the outstanding unpaid balance rather than on the original amount of the loan. Although competition with the profit-making personal finance companies compelled them to quote their rates in monthly rather than in yearly terms, they were strongly in favor of the yearly rate and wanted legislation that would make it universal, thus removing the competitive pressure upon them to quote the deceptive monthly rates.

The industrial unions, notably those in automobiles, steel and clothing, were enthusiastic and helpful supporters. They showed a real awareness of the problems which union members and their families faced as consumers, and put political strength and muscle behind our efforts. The highly idealistic, although lamentably weak, consumers' groups also helped us to their full capacity. As the battle went on year after year, the press began to take notice and new allies appeared. Hillel Black published his extremely well-written little book, *Buy Now, Pay Later,* which had a wide circulation. The Mutual Savings Banks of the Northeast, which had over $50 billion of deposits and which have always been run with a high standard of honor, became convinced that we were right and gave us their support. It was obvious that we were gaining. But as we did so, the opposition redoubled its efforts. The department stores and mail order houses, which had developed a huge business in revolving credit at 1½ percent a month, were very much opposed to admitting that this came to 18 percent a year.

Senator Robertson became even more determined in his opposition and was strongly supported by the ranking Republican, Senator Wallace F. Bennett of Utah. The familiar bipartisan coalition was aroused and in full operation. In addition, inroads were being made among the Northern Democrats. One Senator was quite open in his opposition, and two more refused support unless revolving credit was exempted. Eminent law firms with great political influence as New and Fair Dealers actively entered the fight on the side of the opposition. I presume their fees were not insignificant.

Senators Proxmire of Wisconsin and Maurine Neuberger of Oregon were our two chief supporters, but on any showdown we could not muster a majority.

As we moved into 1966, Senator Neuberger to our regret decided not to run for re-election, and I found myself engaged in a hard race in which I was very decisively defeated. So far as I could determine, my battle for truth-in-lending had brought me very little popular support, while it further marshaled virtually all of the commercial credit industry and the business community against me.

It was personally a heavy political liability which I was glad to bear. But in the curious way in which American political life operates, the idea itself was obviously making headway. The Canadian province of Nova Scotia passed a good law in 1966. Massachusetts had been shaken by scandals involving the bribery of public officials by officers of several personal loan companies, including the two largest. These practices ultimately resulted in the conviction on criminal charges of the companies and their agents as well as of the public official involved. A devoted group of citizens led by Father McEwen of Boston College took advantage of this situation to push for the passage of a strong truth-in-lending act and amidst general surprise, the legislature passed it. Former opponents simply could not stand lining up again as antagonists.

Inside the Senate other changes were happening. Senator Robertson was defeated in the Virginia primaries and his successor, William B. Spong, became a supporter of the bill when he entered the Senate. Senator Robertson's defeat released another Southern vote in the committee which out of regional loyalty had followed him in the past. The new Senator from

Massachusetts, Edward Brooke, had helped to draft the Massachusetts act and was obviously ready to break the solid front of Republican opposition.

Most important of all, Senator Proxmire, who, with my defeat, had moved up to the number-two place on the committee, courageously took up the struggle and reintroduced the bill.

Over in the House, Congresswoman Leonor K. Sullivan of Missouri served notice that if the Senate once passed a bill, she would move in a similar fashion.

The opponents were shaken to find this unexpected turn of events, but they still had a majority of the Senate committee and felt relatively secure.

Some Comments on the History of Interest Rates

Stephen Leacock once said that before a college professor could discuss a subject, he had to go back two thousand years to get a running start. Politicians may be accused of being even more ponderous for drawing on Sidney Homer's classic work, *The History of Interest Rates.* I should like to point out that truth-in-lending legislation is nothing new. For example, over thirty-seven centuries ago, in 1800 B.C., the king of ancient Babylonia decreed that all loans had to be accompanied by a written contract setting forth the terms of the loan. Moreover, if through subterfuge an illegally high rate of interest was actually collected, the principal of the loan was to be forfeited to the borrower. From this evidence, one can only conclude that the truth-in-lending bill is one of the most conservative proposals ever made. In fact, it seems rather strange that the bill has not been championed by those conservative groups who customarily look to the past for complete guidance on the problems of today and tomorrow.

It should also be pointed out that interest gouging has enjoyed an equally long, though not honorable, history. In ancient Greece, loan sharks in Athens are known to have charged interest at the rate of 48 percent a month, or 576 percent a year. And in the fifteenth century, Italian bankers charged the king of France 100 percent interest on a war loan while local merchants were borrowing at only 5 percent. Apparently, the king of France was not considered to be a good credit risk. I cannot help but wonder whether Charles de Gaulle could have done better.

During the Middle Ages, the Catholic Church gradually evolved the just-price doctrine with respect to lending. This held that an interest rate of more than 6 percent was usurious. The Church correctly felt that ordinary citizens seeking so-called consumers' loans to meet expenses caused by births, deaths, accidents, sickness, marriage, and other expenditures where the need for added cash was great, were at a disadvantage in dealing with sophisticated moneylenders and needed the special protection afforded by the just-price doctrine.

The historical and moral sanctity given to the magic figure of 6 percent has survived through the centuries and has found its way into most of our state usury laws. Of course, the "buy now, pay later" plan was virtually unheard of in the Middle Ages, and it would be unrealistic to expect many to make a profit at 6 percent in today's consumer credit market. Nevertheless, the reverent attitude accorded the historic 6 percent still survives, and many lenders take great pains to disguise the fact they are charging more. The so-called time-price doctrine was in fact developed to hide this very fact.

Growth of the Consumer Credit Industry

Borrowing by consumers was frowned upon for a long period of our history. When we lived in a simple rural-agricultural society, the need for consumer credit was not great. The prudent man always paid cash and lived off the farm when times were bad. However, the rapid growth of a modern industrial society and the rise of an urban, wage-earning class has changed the old precepts about credit. Workers needed to borrow money to tide them over periods of unemployment. The growth of a mass production industry in consumption goods required new sources of financing, particularly in articles of a relatively durable and costly nature. However, the very usury laws that had been devised to protect the consumer during the Middle Ages operated to his disadvantage during the latter part of the nineteenth century and the early part of the twentieth.

At a rate of 6 percent, it simply was not possible to attract responsible capital into the costly field of consumer credit. The average size of the loan was small; hence the ratio of fixed processing costs to total costs was high. Risks were greater and the installment plan increased the administrative expense. As a result, the field of consumer credit was abandoned to the illegal loan sharks who frequently charged between 200 and 300 percent a year.

Because of the growing concern over the shocking practices of the loan sharks, the Russell Sage Foundation studied the problem around 1910, and in 1916 drafted a uniform small-loan act as a guide for state action. The model act established a licensed small-loan industry and provided for an interest ceiling of 3½ percent a month on the unpaid balance. It is significant to note that the sponsors expressed the rate ceiling in monthly rather than yearly terms. On a yearly basis, a 3½ percent monthly rate comes to 42 percent. This was probably necessary in order to sell the plan to state legislatures, who still believed in the 6 percent myth. As one careful student put it, "The traumatic effect of a statement of finance charge at an annual rate well above 6 percent would have almost guaranteed that the proposed remedial legislation would not have passed state legislatures and would have shocked the consumer into the arms of the loan shark." * Today forty-nine states have small-loan laws patterned after the Russell Sage Foundation's recommendations.

I well remember a conversation with friends of mine who were setting up what they termed a model small-loans company under one of these laws, saying the business would be at once lucrative and philanthropic. I remarked to them that I had heard of philanthropy at 6 percent but I found it hard to contemplate philanthropy at 42 percent. It may well be true, however, that if the real rate of interest had been stated, it would have been originally impossible to displace the loan sharks, who actually charged a much higher rate.

At about the same time, a second institution arose to meet the needs of consumer credit—industrial banks. Arthur Morris, the founder of the first industrial or Morris-plan bank in 1910, hit upon an ingenious method of avoiding the restrictive features of the usury ceilings. The essence of the Morris plan was to discount a loan at the legal interest rate, while requiring the borrower to establish a separate savings account on which no interest was paid. The savings were then used to pay off the loans and in effect amounted to installment repayments. The courts co-operated by holding that the loan and the savings were separate transactions. Since the consumer paid 6 percent interest on the original face value of the note but only had effective use of the money for approximately half the period, the true annual rate was roughly double the disclosed rate. In addition, separate "service fees" were tacked on, which increased the true rate to 17 or 18 percent. This became known as the "discount plus fee" system and was copied by the commercial banks when they moved into the installment credit field during the 1930's. The co-operative

* Robert W. Johnson, *Methods of Stating Consumer Finance Charges*, p. 29.

credit unions, on the other hand, copied the monthly rate system but at a low maximum of 1 percent a month on the actual amounts owed.

Retail merchants selling under the installment plan came up with still another rate—the "add-on rate." This is similar to the discount method except that the percentage is computed on the principal amount rather than the entire amount of the note. For example, a consumer borrowing $100 under a 6 percent discount would receive $94 and pay back $100. Under a 6 percent add-on contract, he would receive $100 and pay back $106. The true annual rates in both cases are approximately double the declared rate since the borrower has the effective use, averaged out, of only about half the principal, as a result of the periodic repayments. The discount rate, however, is actually more than the corresponding add-on rate, since the amount actually loaned is less and the difference increases with the length of the contract. But both the discount and add-on rate as quoted are roughly one-half of the true annual rate, since they are based upon the original principal rather than the periodically declining balance. For this reason, the Federal Trade Commission prevented the General Motors Acceptance Corporation from advertising a 6 percent add-on rate as 6 percent. The FTC held that most people took this to be 6 percent simple interest, comparable to the interest earned on a savings account. In fact, the simple annual rate is nearly double, or 10.9 percent. This decision of the FTC was later upheld by the U.S. Circuit Court of Appeals.

We have therefore seen that each new method of providing consumer credit bears a similar history. The common elements may be summarized as follows:

1. A need for consumer credit arose which was not being met through existing institutions.

2. It was economically impossible to provide such credit within the 6 percent usury ceilings.

3. It was politically impossible to get state legislatures to recognize explicitly rates above 6 percent.

4. Various methods were therefore developed to raise the effective ceiling while maintaining the appearance of staying within 6 percent.

5. When legal ceilings were set in such a manner, it became common for lenders to advertise and quote their rates in a similar fashion.

The end result has been that the consumer is caught in a veritable jungle of figures. He is unable to make simple and direct comparisons between alternative sources of credit.

The Organized Confusion of Credit

Today there are three principal methods of stating a finance rate—the monthly system, the add-on system and the discount system. Each of these can be drastically modified by charging separate additional fees, which are not counted in the rate. The permutations and combinations are infinite. For example, the loan-shark industry in Texas nearly came under state regulation in 1963. During frantic debates in the state legislature, the loan-shark interests proposed an incredibly complicated system for setting maximum rates. They wanted a legal ceiling of a 10 percent add-on rate, plus a two-dollar monthly service charge for the first six months, plus 0.75 percent each month thereafter. Someone pointed out this could come to a true annual rate of 245 percent on a small loan. "So much the worse for the reformer" was the loan-shark industry's attitude.[*]

None of the rate methods now in use are comparable either

[*] *Texas Observer,* February 21, 1963.

with each other or with the simple annual rate on the declining balance which would be most familiar to borrowers. The simple annual rate is the rate earned on savings accounts and the rate paid on home mortgages. It is the rate used by businessmen in commercial transactions and in money markets. Businessmen demand a statement of the true annual rate when they borrow. Sophisticated economists and mathematicians who work for large corporations insist that the simple annual rate be disclosed on all investments and business borrowings. It is only in the field of consumer credit that confusion and obfuscation prevail. Here borrowers are being forced to pay interest on amounts they have already repaid. They are not told this, however. In fact, this is carefully concealed from them.

When the consumer is faced with this jungle of rate methods and complicated financial terms, it is no wonder that he frequently throws up his hands and asks merely to see the size of the monthly payments. For unless he is a skilled mathematician, he will be utterly confused and thoroughly misled if he attempts to compare the rates quoted by various lenders.

The American consumer has been bewildered and numbed by this confusion in credit and, as a result, has been educated not to be price conscious. One recent study asked a sample of eight hundred families to estimate the rate of interest they were actually paying on their debts. The average estimate was 8.3 percent. The actual rate was nearly three times higher, or 23.2 percent.*

In recent years a further abuse of consumer credit has developed, namely, the avoidance of quoting any price at all on many consumer durables and instead merely stating that the purchaser is supposed to pay x dollars for y months. This is the common practice on secondhand autos and is not unusual even on new cars. It is quite frequently used in the purchase

* Juster and Shay, *Consumer Sensitivity to Finance Rates*, 1964, p. 51.

of furniture, washing machines and other laundry appliances, television and radio sets, etc. This practice has even begun to penetrate the field of consumer perishables or soft goods. In these cases, both the price and the interest rate are concealed. It is important that they be brought out into the open, and this the truth-in-lending bills were aimed to do. The bills provided a disclosure that would require (1) computation of interest on the amounts actually owed and not on the amounts already repaid, (2) quotation of these interest rates to consumers on a yearly basis and not primarily on the deceptive monthly basis, (3) quotation of the price of the article as well as the total credit charge in dollars and percent and (4) quotation of special charges incident to the credit transaction, to be included in the percentage finance rates.

The ironic climax to our struggles came in the argument advanced by the credit industry for perpetuating the status quo—that the consumers' lack of concern over rates, which is in large part due to the confusion the lenders themselves have created, is full justification for maintaining the present state of confusion. This is roughly analogous to the logic employed in the Salem witch trials, where the silence of the accused was held to be clear evidence of their guilt.

As a matter of fact, it is relatively easy to find the approximate annual interest rate on the unpaid balance. At least two financial services have prepared rate books giving these rates on loans of varying amounts for varying periods of time. The Bowery Savings Bank of New York has produced a cheap and simple slide rule enabling buyers and borrowers to find the approximate true annual rate, while the Credit Union National Association has developed an inexpensive circular slide rule that will permit both sellers and lenders to state the rate correctly to the nearest tenth of a percent. Both of these were familiar to those members of the committee who attended the hearings in former years. In the final stages of the struggle,

Mr. Cedric Kroll of the Treasury showed that even irregular payments could be reduced to a formula and made clear.

As a matter of fact, there are four interrelated variables, and from any three of them the fourth can be computed.

These are: (1) the original cash purchase price, (2) the number of months over which the payments are made, (3) the amount in dollars to be paid each month and (4) the annual rate of interest. Once 1, 2 and 3 are given, 4 can be found. Today the lender or seller on the installment plan generally has a rate book under the table that enables him to find the amount of the monthly payment according to the price, the number of months and the true rate of interest.

Frequently the seller now decides what interest rate he wants to charge, and then, on the basis of the other two variables, he quotes the monthly payments required. It would be just as easy to find the interest rate once the other variables are stated, as our bills would have required.

The Size of the Credit Industry

By any standards, consumer credit today is, as we have seen, big business. In the spring of 1968 the American consumer owed slightly over $100 billion in short- and intermediate-term debt. Interest payments alone on this debt amounted to at least $12 billion and probably much more.

The rate of growth is also instructive. Since 1945, consumer credit has increased from $5.6 billion to $100 billion, or by eighteen times. The growth rate of consumer debt was four and one-half times greater than the growth rate of our gross national product (GNP). We are sometimes told that government finance is no different from family finance and that the federal government should manage its fiscal affairs as though it were a family. Yet if we actually did this—if during the post-war years we had actually increased the national debt at the same rate by which American families increased theirs—the size of the national debt today would be over *four trillion dollars*, a truly incomprehensible figure.

I do not cite these figures in criticism or mean to imply that the volume of consumer credit is too high. I do believe, however, that the sheer size of consumer debt and its rapid rate of growth have great significance for our economy. No one really knows what is the proper level of consumer debt. But when it has reached the unprecedented size that it has, I believe we should do all we can to insure the proper use of credit. Consumers themselves are in the long run the best judges of how much credit they can afford, but when the cost of credit is obscured, this self-adjusting mechanism is frustrated. Certainly the continued increase in personal bankruptcies indicates that some consumers cannot manage credit. In fact, the trade publications of the credit industry are filled with articles deploring the number of people forced into bankruptcy. I don't know why it has never occurred to the credit industry that one way of reducing the number of these bankruptcies is to make people aware of the real cost of credit. Instead of opposing truth in lending, it seems to me that the credit industry should support it in its own economic self-interest. I believe it would reduce the number of defaults. It is important that drivers should know the rate of speed at which their autos are going. It is equally important that borrowers should know the rate of interest which they are paying.

The size of consumer debt and its rate of growth indicate the magnitude of the savings that would be made possible by restoring price competition in the consumer credit industry. If, as a result of vigorous price competition, the average rate of interest on consumer debt declined by only one percentage point, American families would save about one billion dollars a year! Most of these savings would go to the poor, who can least afford to be in debt. Thus, the economic potential of truth in lending is considerable. Moreover, the savings to consumers would become larger every year, considering the rapid rate of growth of consumer credit. If consumer credit maintains its annual growth rate of 14.4 percent, a saving of one billion dollars per year would nearly double in slightly over five years.

Most of the ostensible objections have centered on the workability of disclosing a simple annual rate. Numerous examples of irregular transactions were presented where the computation of the simple annual rate was alleged to be difficult. I believe the experience under the Massachusetts Truth-in-Lending Law and the Department of Defense (DOD) directive will show how groundless these objections are. For the vast majority of transactions, the disclosure of a true annual rate will be ridiculously easy, and there is no reason why the few irregular transactions couldn't be dealt with in separate procedures established by the administering agency with the assistance of the credit industry. If the credit industry was unwilling to trust the Federal Reserve Board to write workable regulations, the industry should have proposed detailed amendments to the bill covering the methods by which irregular payment plans would be handled. Yet the facts of the matter are that for seven long years the industry maintained a completely negative and unco-operative attitude. Never once did they come forward with any language suggesting how the bill could be made more workable. From this evidence, one can only conclude that the question of irregular payment plans has been used as a red herring to confuse the issue. Mr. Kroll has finally resolved the theoretical difficulties on this point.

The real reasons for the opposition to truth in lending have been not technical but, rather, psychological. Creditors have apparently feared that a disclosure of the true rate of interest will alienate consumers. According to this view, if consumers once knew the rate they were paying for credit, they would resent the credit industry so much that they would decrease their borrowing and buying.

I would make the same reply to this objection that Stephen Leacock once made to the assertion of his friend, a professor of Classics, that the study of Greek had made him what he was. "This," rejoined Leacock, "is a very grave charge if true."

To say that the real interest rates are so high that they cannot stand the light of day would certainly be a grave charge. Perhaps there should be a revolt, but I know of no evidence that there will be.

What truth in lending would actually do would be to stimulate meaningful price competition. And it is precisely this that most of the lending industry wishes to avoid. The disclosure of the annual rate will make consumers more aware of the actual differences in the cost of credit. Some rates running, for example, from 40 percent to even higher figures will not stand up under publicity, and consumers will shift to lenders charging lower rates. Now it has become an economic fact of life that despite lip service to the principle of free enterprise, almost no business likes to compete in terms of price. Every industry tries on the contrary to avoid price competition as much as possible. So it is natural that when public policy attempts to foster greater price competition, such proposals are vehemently opposed. Banks in particular should gain from a revelation of the true rates, since their rates are below those of the alternative credit sources. I believe that the violent past opposition of the American Bankers' Association has been due in part to a failure to recognize where its members' legitimate interests lie.

There also seems to be an inherent tendency on the part of American business to grossly overestimate the adverse impact of reform legislation while ignoring almost entirely

the benefits to the general public and the ultimate benefit to
business. When Congress passed the Truth-in-Securities Act
of 1933, the President of the New York Stock Exchange
solemnly predicted the collapse of the market. Today the
stock market is stronger than ever and rests in large part upon
the public confidence made possible by the Truth-in-Securities
Act. It should always be remembered that the American
Bankers Association also fought the coming of the Federal
Reserve System with great bitterness and the utmost vigor
and vehemence. Now the bankers are its strongest supporters
and seem to believe they originated it. They also fiercely
fought federal deposit insurance for funds deposited in banks.
Today deposit insurance is the bulwark of the banking industry. Bankers would be horrified if anyone even hinted that
federal deposit insurance should be repealed.

Similar opposition was expressed toward full-disclosure
legislation dealing with wool products, furs, textiles, auto
prices, and truth in packaging. In all of these cases, the fears
of the industry failed to materialize. Sales were not reduced;
on the contrary, they increased, helped in part by greater
confidence.

I believe the same will hold true for truth in lending. The
credit industry seems to suffer from a massive inferiority
complex, which leads them to overreact against reforms proposed by others. We have seen that the confusion about pre-
senting finance charges is due to circumstances that existed
fifty years ago. A departure from the simple annual rate concept, which had been used throughout four thousand years of
history, was thought to be necessary in order to get around the
usury laws and persuade state legislatures to authorize the
establishment of a responsible credit industry.

Today, all of the earlier legal and political difficulties have
been overcome. The credit industry is no longer struggling to
get started—it is large and prosperous. People are more

sophisticated about credit and are no longer likely to rise up in anger over the death of the "6 percent myth." Responsible creditors have nothing to fear from telling the public the truth, and I should think that from the standpoint of good public relations, they ought to have taken the lead in supporting such legislation.

The Function of an Annual Rate

Since most of the objections to this bill have centered upon the disclosure of an annual rate, the value of this information needs to be made clear. Some in the industry, for example, have argued that consumers need only a statement of the cost of credit in dollars and cents. According to this view, comparison among different credit plans can be made in dollar terms. It is held that dollar comparisons are more meaningful to the consumer because he spends dollars, not percents.

This is effective rhetoric but poor logic. A rate is essentially a standard unit price for the rental of money. If unit prices were eliminated in marketing, the consumer would be at a loss to make effective comparisons. Just as a price per gallon of gasoline or a price per quart of milk or a price per pound of steak is useful to the consumer, so would a standard unit price for money be useful.

Let me illustrate this point with a concrete example. Suppose you want to buy a car on time and that, after negotiating the down-payment and trade-in allowance with the dealer, you are left with a balance of $2,300 to finance. Suppose the dealer is willing to finance the car over 36 months and quotes a total finance charge of $362.25. Is this a good credit buy? Most people couldn't really tell without extensive computation.

Suppose you are wary and decide to shop around. Perhaps

a bank is willing to lend you the money, but it might require a higher down-payment and lend only for 24 months. Thus, the bank might lend you $1,900 for 24 months at a total finance charge of $285.00. Is this better than the car dealer's terms? The dollar cost is cheaper, but the term is shorter and the amount of the loan is smaller. Does one offset the other? The fact of the matter is that most people couldn't tell for sure. As soon as the concept of an annual finance rate is introduced, the matter becomes clear. In the case of the car dealer, the rate comes to 9.76 percent, while the deal offered by the bank comes to 13.80 percent.

Dollars by themselves do not tell the whole story. It is impossible to make an adequate comparison only on the basis of dollars when the amounts of the down-payment or length of the contract are varied. Thus, the notion that consumers can intelligently shop around without information on the rate of the finance charges is simply not true. The rate is indispensable for intelligent choice, just as a knowledge of speeds is for intelligent driving.

The rate serves another function in addition to comparison shopping. It tells a buyer whether he ought to shop around in the first place. Let us return to the previous example of a car loan. If the buyer knew in advance the rate was only 9.76 percent, he would know instantly that he was getting a pretty good buy on credit. He wouldn't have to waste his time in calling up or visiting other creditors and negotiating terms. He could confidently complete his transaction with the first car dealer without the gnawing suspicion that he was being taken on the credit charge.

On the other hand, suppose you started with a different car dealer, who quoted a finance charge of $600.00 on an unpaid balance of $2,000.00 over 18 months. Is this a good buy? The rate would provide the answer. It comes to 35.05 percent. The rate would tell you immediately that you had better look elsewhere for credit. You are not likely to be mis-led by the salesman's bland assurance that you are getting a good credit buy.

Thus, the rate permits a consumer immediately to recognize a good buy, thereby saving his time; and it permits him to recognize immediately a bad buy, thereby saving his money.

The true annual rate has a third function from the point of view of the consumer. It helps him decide whether he wants to use credit at all or to use cash. Since the rate is a true annual rate, it is directly comparable to the rate earned in a savings account or the rate that would be paid by borrowing on a life insurance policy. It is also comparable to the rate paid on a home mortgage.

It is sometimes argued that most consumers do not have the option of using cash or other liquid assets. However, a careful study by the University of Michigan Survey Research Center * found the following:

1. Roughly one-third of spending units with debt could have eliminated their entire personal debt had they chosen to substitute some of their liquid assets for going in debt.

2. An additional one-third could have reduced a portion of their debt by substituting their liquid assets.

3. If this had been done, the savings in interest would have been widely distributed among income groups and would not have been confined only to the wealthy.

A further study indicates that those who do hold liquid assets are somewhat more inclined to borrow less when rates go up and vice versa than those who don't own liquid assets. Thus, knowledge of the rate is important if this tendency is to be realized.†

* "1959 Survey of Consumer Finances," *Federal Reserve Bulletin,* July 1959.
† Juster and Shay, *Consumer Sensitivity to Finance Rates,* 1964, p. 38.

Thus, the true annual rate plays three indispensable functions:

1. It provides a simple yardstick for comparison shopping.
2. It permits immediate recognition of good and bad buys.
3. It affords a direct comparison with the alternative of using liquid assets.

The Economic Rationale for Disclosing an Annual Rate

Aside from protecting the average person on individual credit transactions, the annual rate provision has an economic significance that may be even greater in public benefit.

First of all, a rate is, as I have said, like a price. Thus, when creditors are required to display their prices it is bound to have an impact. Buyers will become price-conscious. Creditors will begin to compete in terms of price. The over-all aggregate effect may be to lower rates throughout the entire credit industry. As I have indicated, a reduction in the rate of one percentage point could save consumers a billion dollars a year. It is sometimes argued that buyers don't care about rates and that rate disclosure would have no appreciable effect on competition. The answer to this claim is twofold:

First, many buyers are not sensitive to rates because of the hopeless confusion surrounding consumer credit. The introduction of a uniform method of stating finance rates will make it possible to educate most consumers to be "rate-conscious," i.e., price-conscious. Present educational efforts are frustrated by the lack of rate information and the practice of quoting rates in many different ways.

Second, even if after education most consumers should still ignore rates, all would not be lost. It takes only a small minority of price-conscious shoppers to police a market and force sellers to compete on price. Thus, the disclosure of annual rates can lead to price competition even if a majority of the buyers ignore the rates.

By restoring price competition in credit, the disclosure of annual rate will tend to bring about a more equitable collection of credit charges among different groups. It will work to change the present situation, where the poor, the uneducated, and disadvantaged minority groups subsidize the rich and well-educated. Let me illustrate this point with another example.

Car dealers frequently make more money on the finance charges than they do on the car. It is common practice for a sales finance company to kick back a portion of the finance charge to the dealer. What many dealers do is to reduce the cash price of the car to make a sale, and make up the loss in the finance charge. Competition works in the sale of the car because buyers are well informed about price. But it does not work in the field of credit because buyers are not informed about the price of credit or the true interest rate.

Thus the cash buyer or the buyer who is informed enough to borrow elsewhere obtains a good deal. He is able to buy a car far cheaper than it would cost him if the dealer's fair profit were added in. The difference is made up by the credit buyer who may lack education or have no access to other forms of credit. Thus, the poor subsidize the rich.

However, if we separate the market for the car and the market for credit, we will restore price competition in both markets and end this unconscionable subsidy. I am not charging that creditors deliberately discriminate against the poor. But I do say that the lack of price competition on credit inevitably works against the poor. It is the system that must be changed. The poor do pay more, for credit as well as for commodities.

A further economic benefit from increased price competition is an improved allocation of resources within the credit industry. To the extent that price competition is absent, high cost and inefficient lenders are permitted to survive and grow. Price competition, on the other hand, will divert resources to the more efficient lenders at a consequent saving to the public. But if price competition is to function, the annual rate must be disclosed to permit ready comparisons of unit costs. How could gasoline dealers achieve meaningful price competition if they refused to disclose the price per gallon of gasoline?

Another economic benefit to be derived from truth in lending is an improved allocation of resources between liquid assets and credit. To the extent that consumers reduce liquid assets as an alternative to increasing their debt, they are substituting a low-cost form of borrowing for a high-cost form. Thus, they will be able to save the difference in interest payments to apply to additional purchases. However, full knowledge of the rate being charged for credit is necessary if this optimum is to be reached.

The basic philosophy behind truth in lending is fundamentally a belief in free enterprise and in the price system. But if markets are to function properly, there must be a free flow of information. Perfect competition requires perfect information. Of course, perfect competition does not exist anywhere in our economy. Nevertheless, it is an ideal towards which public policy should work. By removing imperfections and frictions, we permit free markets to achieve their maximum effect. By increasing the amount of information on consumer credit, we will remove a major imperfection in the market place.

The alternative to regulation by the market is regulation by the government. This is generally less efficient and leads to an increase in governmental power, which conservatives deplore. It is always a source of ironical wonder to me when I so commonly find the verbal supporters of free enterprise opposing reforms that would lead to greater disclosure and more competition. That is what they did so overwhelmingly in this case.

The Final Struggle

I left the legislative story at the point where popular opinion in favor of truth-in-lending was growing. It was beginning to permeate the Senate Banking and Currency Committee, although that body was still basically antagonistic. After a hard struggle, Senator Proxmire was able to get a fairly strong bill reported out of the committee. But so vigorous was the opposition of the mail-order companies, the department stores and other mercantile interests that in order to get his majority, he had to exempt a large portion of revolving credit from disclosing an annual rate and to promise that no effort would be made to strengthen the bill on the floor. With this understanding the bill then sailed through the Senate by a unanimous vote. This permitted many deathbed converts who had opposed the measure for eight long years to go before the public and proudly point to their vote as proof of their devotion to truth-in-lending.

Some have criticized Senator Proxmire for conceding on most of revolving credit. I do not. It was the minimum price which he had to pay to get any bill at all. I have never been opposed to a compromise if it is necessary. But I am opposed to yielding prematurely and excessively. In Senator Proxmire's place, I would have followed the same course. As a matter of fact, he kept the bill alive and in a relatively healthy state.

The bill then moved to the House with the full support of the Administration. Everyone expected that the legislative process would water it down still further. But they reckoned without Congresswoman Leonore Sullivan. For years she and her devoted staff had been studying the whole credit situation as it affected low- and moderate-income folk. She now moved into attack and produced an alternative which strengthened rather than weakened the bill. All of revolving credit was restored, so that the 1½-percent-a-month firms were now required to tell the truth, and if newspaper ads contained any financial terms, the creditor was also required to state the true annual rate. Most daring of all, Mrs. Sullivan struck directly at the abuses in wage garnishment. As finally agreed upon, creditors cannot garnish more than 25 percent of a person's after-tax pay, but at least $48 a week is immune from seizure. Employers were prohibited from discharging employees solely because of a single garnishment. I had never dared contemplate such much needed provisions lest I lose the whole bill. But with all colors flying, the undaunted Congresswoman swept ahead. She outlawed with criminal penalties the so-called "Shylock" or "juice" loans of the underworld.

For the main features of the bill, the Federal Reserve Board was to establish standards and each government financial agency was to enforce the standards for the private institutions under their jurisdiction. The Federal Trade Commission, however, was to enforce compliance among all other creditors, including finance companies and retail merchants. The Department of Labor would enforce the wage-garnishment provisions.

The Republicans were so taken aback by the Sullivan move that they decided not to fight the bill as passed by the Senate. They now introduced it as their bill. With the aid of Democratic defections induced by mercantile pressures, they succeeded in defeating some of the Sullivan amendments both in sub-committee and in the full committee. Congressman Halpern of the minority, however, as an honorable exception worked hard for the Sullivan version.

Mrs. Sullivan, with the help of Chairman Patman, then carried the fight to the floor. Few gave her any chance. But by one of the most moving speeches in years, she carried the House with her and so shamed the opposition that she almost literally drove them from the floor. Only twenty-nine finally dared to rise in opposition. Joan of Arc herself could not have done better.

Then came the final struggle in conference. Mrs. Sullivan controlled the House conferees and Proxmire gave her every assistance on the Senate side. At first, however, the majority of the Senate conferees refused to yield. The conferees were deadlocked for six long and tumultuous sessions. Finally a face-saving compromise on revolving credit was engineered which permitted a Democrat to give ground and to accept the main features of the Sullivan bill. Both houses then ratified the agreement and the President signed the Proxmire-Sullivan bill into law amidst general approval. A group of consumers without either money or political power had defeated the financial, mercantile, industrial and legal élite of the nation. The humble had demonstrated that they could win if their cause was righteous and if they persisted.

The act had demonstrated two other reassuring peculiarities. It had been a measure initiated in and by Congress and not by the Executive Branch, and it had been kept alive and strengthened by members of Congress. The White House in the later stages had been very helpful, but it was Congress's bill. Secondly, it was one of those rare bills which was much stronger when passed than when introduced. The early decisions not to agree to weakening provisions were therefore vindicated by events.

The period of agitation is over. The era of administration is beginning. Let us hope that the measure can survive the rocks and shoals of these difficulties and that popular interest may hold the enforcing officers to a fidelity in their task.*

---

* I cannot let this occasion pass without paying tribute to some of the devoted men and women who made the victory possible and whose names are never mentioned. First, the staff members who did so much patient and path-breaking work: Milton Semer, Jonathan Lindley, Kenneth E. Gray, Kenneth McLean and Howard Shuman

In conclusion, may I quote from a poem by Alfred Noyes, which I hope may be appropriate to the issue:

> I caught the fire from those who went before,
> The bearers of the torch who could not see
> The goal to which they strained. I caught their fire,
> And carried it, only a little way beyond;
> But there are those who wait for it, I know,
> Those who will carry it on to victory.

---

on the Senate side and Charles Holstein, the devoted and able assistant to Congresswoman Sullivan. Then the men and women from diverse groups who helped to distribute information and arouse informed public opinion, such as Oren Shipe and George Meyers of the credit-union movement, Grover Ensley, Morris Crawford and William McKenna of the Mutual Savings Banks. Sarah Newman of the Consumers' League, Andrew Biemiller, Kenneth Meiklejohn and Kenneth Young of the A.F.L.-C.I.O., Jack Sheehan of the Steelworkers, Evelyn Dubrow of the I.L.G.W.U. and Jane O'Grady of the Amalgamated Clothing Workers, Arnold Mayer of the Meat Cutters Union, David Cohen, Jacob Clayman and Marvin Kaplan of the I.U.D., Dan Bedell and Frank Wallick of the U.A.W. and many others, such as Dr. Richard Morse of Kansas State University, Father R. J. McEwen of Boston College, and John Edleman of the National Council of Senior Citizens. We are grateful also to Esther Peterson, Assistant Secretary of Labor, Betty Furness, the consumers' representative in the office of the President, Robert Wallace, Assistant Secretary of the Treasury, Joseph Barr, the Under-Secretary of the Treasury and Cedric Kroll, the Government's Actuary. The devoted workers in Massachusetts and Canada also helped to swell the tide which moved towards victory.

And I wish to record our especial gratitude to Herbert E. Cheever, a public-spirited and honorable banker, now located in California but who as a South Dakotan became indignant at the practices in the field of consumer credit and dared to come to Washington to testify and to brave the wrath of his fellow bankers.

But most of all we are grateful for the way in which the great American public, so often deceived and misled, finally saw what was involved and responded to the occasion.

5

The Extent and
Contours of Poverty

Six years ago Michael Harrington wrote an extraordinary little book called *The Other America* on the forgotten poor of our nation. This book and a review of it by Dwight MacDonald in *The New Yorker* in early 1963 helped to waken the conscience of many people.

Largely inspired by these writings, President Kennedy then planned a war on poverty and President Johnson has tried to carry it out. The passage of the Economic Opportunity Act of 1965 and its administration has widened the area of national concern. It has made the question of poverty and its reduction one of the basic issues of the day. There is no longer the same complacency that had been previously en-

couraged by the increase in our national prosperity and by
at least the title, if not by all the contents, of John Kenneth
Galbraith's excellent book *The Affluent Society*. And the Poor
People's Campaign has given further emphasis to the existence
of poverty amidst plenty.

One of the first questions to be answered was: Who are
the poor and how many are they? The Council of Economic
Advisers began by fixing a rough minimum income for a
city family of four at $3,000 a year and made this the di-
viding line. Those below this figure were regarded as "poor"
and those above the line as "not poor." The Office of Economic Opportunity then computed a still lower level, $2,000,
as the line below which a family could be considered to be
in "abject poverty." Since then, the Social Security Administration, through an extremely able statistician, Miss Mollie Orshansky, and with the co-operation of the Census Bureau,
has worked out more detailed minimum budgets and the approximate numbers and proportion who could properly be
said to be poor.* Building on a minimum food budget from
the Department of Agriculture,† Miss Orshansky estimated
that in 1963 each person in a nonfarm family of four would
need 70 cents a day to be properly fed. Then, from a study
of existing budgets, she concluded that at least one-third
of such a poverty budget would go for food and that, therefore, $1.40 a day would be required for all other items in the
budget from housing to clothing, medicine, household operation, carfare and incidentals. This made a daily total of $2.10
a person and fixed the "poverty line" in 1963 at $3,130 for a
nonfarm family of four. By 1966, the food budget of the De-

---

* Mollie Orshansky, "Counting the Poor," *Social Security Bulletin*,
January 1965, pp. 3–29; "Who's Who Among the Poor," *ibid.*, July
1965, pp. 3–32. See other articles by her in the same journal for
April, May and December 1966, and, particularly, her article "The
Shape of Poverty in 1966," *ibid.*, March 1968, pp. 3–32.
† See *Family Food Plans and Food Costs*, Home Economics Association
Report No. 20, U.S. Department of Agriculture, 1962.

partment of Agriculture came to 75 cents a day or $3.00 for a family of four. Estimating total costs as three times this figure, a poverty level of $2.25 a day for each person was fixed. This came to a yearly total for 1966 of $3,335, or about $65 a week. This was an increase of 7 percent over 1963, which roughly corresponds to the increase in the cost of living. By the winter of 1968, the needed sum would have been $3,525.

It was obviously necessary to work out minimum totals also for farm families, and for families of different sizes. Since in 1955 about 40 percent of the food requirements of a farm family were raised on the farm itself, it was at first thought that shelter and other facilities offered by the farm would come to an equal percentage. Miss Orshansky then computed that a farm family would need about 60 percent as much in cash as a nonfarm family to maintain the same level of life. For 1963, this was set at approximately $1,860 or $1,900. A later survey of the Department of Agriculture lowered the proportion of a farm family's food that was home grown to 30 percent, so that in the next revision the ratio of farm living costs to urban was raised from 60 to 70 percent. After refining the figures in a very elaborate way for families of different sizes so that children would not be counted as equivalent to fathers and so that the "economies" of larger-size families could be taken into account, Miss Orshansky arrived at the following ratios and amounts, which were probably approximately correct for nonfarm families in 1966.

Size of Family	Amount Needed at Poverty Line	Ratio to Cost for Family of Four
1	$1,635	49
2	$2,115	63
3	$2,600	78
4	$3,335	100
5	$3,930	118
6	$4,410	132
7 or more	$5,430	163

For the winter of 1968, the totals would have been 5.7 percent higher.

Miss Orshansky then made a final improvement. She defined a level of living on the fringes of poverty that would include the "near poor" as well as the "poor." On the basis of actual budgets, she concluded that here the minimum food costs should amount to a quarter rather than a third of the total cost. The total costs for this group were therefore estimated at four times the food costs, or at $2.80 a day per person in a four-member family rather than $2.10. In 1966, this figure had risen to $3 a day for each person. This brought the yearly figure for near-poor nonfarm families in 1963 to $4,200, and to $4,345 in 1966, with the resulting variations for farm families and for families of different sizes in the same ratios as before. Even this was very much below the minimum that had been worked out for city families by the Bureau of Labor Statistics. It was in fact less than half of the $9,100 "moderate" budget which the bureau had suggested during the summer of 1967 for city families of the standard size. These elaborately refined figures agreed roughly with earlier studies by Harrington, MacDonald, Leon Keyserling, and the Council of Economic Advisers, if interim changes in the cost of living are taken into consideration.

Allowing for increases in the cost of living, the cost for the standard family of four can be roughly estimated as follows for March 1966.* For 1967 it would have been 3 percent higher, and for 1968 6 percent higher.

Level	Nonfarm	Farm
abject poverty	$2,225	$1,555
poverty	$3,335	$2,345
economy (near poor)	$4,445	$3,040

* By the winter of 1968, the "abject" poverty figure for the nonfarm family was $2,350 and the upper limit for the near poor $4,750.

There is, of course, a margin of error in all these estimates, which well-paid critics have been quick to point out. The contents of these budgets are certainly far above the general level for India and other parts of Asia, or for Africa and Latin America. The poverty level is, however, only about a third of the "moderate" family budget prepared by the Bureau of Labor Statistics. I suggest that if the critics were to try living on these amounts, instead of carping from lofty economic heights, most of their opposition would dissolve. When judged by American standards, the allowances are not excessive. I am reminded of the reply given to a speech by President Charles W. Eliot of Harvard in which he told a mass meeting of striking motormen how fortunate they were to serve the public. Then came a husky voice from the rear of the room: "Try it yourself, President Eliot, and see how you like it."

The Census Bureau made initially an elaborate sampling study, covering 25,000 families which were grouped according to the ratios of such families in the population as a whole. This was later increased to a sample of 35,000 families, and more recently to one of 50,000. This sample is now taken in over 700 communities and was for some time believed to be an adequate cross section of the American nation. On the basis of this census sampling, the following numbers were estimated by Miss Orshansky and the Census Bureau to be in "poverty" in March of the years covered.

Year	Number in Millions	Percent of Noninstitutional Population
1959–63	35.3	19
1964	34.1	18
1965	32.7	17
1966 *	29.7	15
1967	25.9	13

* While page proofs were being read on this chapter, the Census revised its figure for 1966 to 28.8 million.

Here again the final results check roughly with previous estimates by Robert Lampman, Keyserling, Harrington, Mac-Donald and others. If we include those on the fringes of poverty or the "near poor," we find a total of 51 million for 1963, or 27 percent of the population. By 1966 this had been apparently reduced to about 45 million, or 23 percent of the population of the country.* There was an apparent decrease of 3 million in the boom year of 1966 alone, which was also accompanied by increased efforts to reduce poverty on the part of the national government.

Later, however, from the comparison of birth, death, and immigration statistics with the census totals, it became apparent that the 1950 and 1960 census figures represented a serious undercount of the total population, which means that the poverty estimates based on them were also too low.

Competent census statisticians have estimated that the undercount was as much as 5.7 million in 1950 and 1960, and they have made the same estimate for 1967.† The revised estimates for the total population were therefore 157 million for 1950 (the official figure was 151 million), 185 million for 1960 (official figure, 179 million) and 204 million for 1967. These were 3.6, 3.1, and 2.8 percent respectively more than the official totals.

This undercount was not the fault of the Census Bureau, but was caused by two factors: (1) an unavoidable failure to cover all living quarters and households, (2) the existence of a number who either were absent from home or had no

* See Social Security Administration (Department of Health, Education and Welfare), *The Poor in 1965 and Trends 1959–65*, p. 3. Also Joint Economic Committee, *Coordination and Integration of Government Statistical Programs* (1967), p. 172.

† See Pritzloff and Rotterwell, *Procedural Difficulties in Taking Past Censuses in Predominantly Negro, Puerto Rican and Mexican Areas,* Census Bureau (1967); and Siegal, *Completeness of Coverage of Non-White Population in 1960. Census and Current Estimates,* Census Bureau (1967).

fixed living facilities. The latter were mostly people in the lower depths, who slept in stations, streets and alleys, hallways, all-night movies, automobiles, abandoned houses, etc. These were among the "abjectly poor" but not counted among them. A much larger percentage of such groups as Negroes, Puerto Ricans and Mexican-Americans was admittedly missed than of whites, namely 9½ percent as compared with 2.2 percent, or a ratio of about 4 to 1. In totals it was estimated that the undercount of nonwhites in 1960 was 3.6 million, and of whites 2.1 million.

It is obvious that the persons who were missed were not distributed evenly throughout the different economic layers of the population, but were far more heavily congregated among the poor. While we cannot state exactly the number of the poor who were thus missed, it would not be far wrong to set the minimum at around 2 million.* It may well have been more.

I estimate, therefore, that the number of the poor in 1965 was at least 35 instead of 33 million, and in 1966, close to 32 instead of 29.7 million. This would raise the proportions in poverty by a percentage point above Miss Orshansky's estimates. In 1967 the total would have been around 28 or 29 million.

The total of "poor" and "near poor" would then be close to 47 million in 1966, and to several million less in 1967.

Taking into consideration the numbers found by the various surveys to be in "abject poverty"—living on less than two-thirds of the poverty levels—one can divide the poor and

---

* This is much more than the estimates of the census which allow for an unemployment rate among the uncounted only twice that for the measured population. I believe, on the contrary, that this minimizes the undercount of the poor. It is dangerous to assume, as does the census, that the persons missed were primarily "away from home when the interviewer calls and in occupations which the missing persons may not wish to discuss." There are in fact more persons in the lowest depths and countryside of our cities than many are willing to admit.

near poor into three almost equal groups of from 13 to 14½ millions each: (1) those in "abject poverty"; (2) those in poverty not yet "abject" and (3) those on the fringes of poverty or the "near poor."

Later refinements may be developed, such as the costs in smaller cities and small towns, which are probably less than Miss Orshansky's estimates. But let us rest here for the moment so far as totals are concerned. We know enough to say that the problem of poverty is serious—deadly serious. It cannot be swept under the rug by anyone with a sensitive conscience. We cannot be indifferent when a seventh of the nation are desperately poor and almost a fourteenth are "abjectly poor."

In her earlier studies Miss Orshansky had divided the poor into two main groups, namely those living directly on the farm and those not on the farm. In a later study, she separated the nonfarm group into three main subdivisions: (1) central cities of over 50,000 population within some 223 (now 228) broader metropolitan areas, (2) suburbs and satellite cities in these metropolitan areas (nearly 65 percent of the population lived in these two divisions) and (3) smaller cities and small towns outside the so-called metropolitan areas but not on the farms. The last set of communities includes the smaller trading and manufacturing centers, intermediate between the farms and the metropolitan centers, with a total population of about 55 million. By separating the poor in this fashion, Miss Orshansky obtained comparisons for four geographical divisions instead of for the original two. She found that in 1964 the probable numbers of the poor in each of these areas and the proportions of the totals were as shown in the table on the opposite page.*

These statistics indicate that poverty was greatest where the

* Mollie Orshansky, "The Poor in City and Suburb, 1964," *Social Security Bulletin,* December 1966, pp. 1–16. *Ibid.,* p. 6.

ratio of population to space is least, namely on the farms, where 33 percent or one-third were in poverty. Next came the smaller towns and cities where over a third of the country's poor lived and where approximately a quarter of the total population were "poor." Then came the central cities, where 17 percent or one-sixth were poor.

	Estimated Total Population in Millions (1964)	*Estimated Number of Poor in Millions* (1964)	*% Poor*
Central Cities of Metropolitan Areas	58.6	10.1	17.2
Suburbs & Satellite Cities of Metropolitan Areas	62.6	6.3	10.0
Smaller Cities & Small Towns (Nonmetropolitan)	55.4	13.5	24.4
On Farm	13.3	4.4	32.9
TOTAL	189.9	34.3	18.0

It is thus clear that poverty is neither exclusively nor even primarily a big-city problem. The ratio of the poor in the big cities was, as a matter of fact, only about half what it was on the farms and nearly a third less than in the smaller cities and towns. It is a striking fact that only about 30 percent of those whom Miss Orshansky regarded as poor lived in the big central cities, while approximately half lived on the farms and in the small towns and cities intermediate between countryside and metropolis.

As was to be expected, poverty was least prevalent in the suburbs of the big metropolitan areas. Here Miss Orshansky was unable to differentiate between the industrial satellites such as Yonkers in the New York complex and the residential suburbs such as Hartsdale and Scarsdale. Similarly, in the

Chicago area, Chicago Heights and Waukegan could not be differentiated from Lake Forest, Kenilworth and Glen Ellyn. The combined average was 10 percent. But if it had been possible to separate the totals, the industrial suburbs would have been shown to have had a much higher percentage than the residential suburbs. The residential suburbs, or bedroom communities, are in a sense somewhat segregated communities, segregated by wealth and color from direct contact with the poor and those of darker skins.

The general results obtained by Miss Orshansky and the Census Bureau will, in all probability, hold up under close analysis. But they probably do somewhat overstate the actual amount of poverty outside the metropolitan areas. This is because living costs are probably not so high in the small towns and smaller cities as in Miss Orshansky's definition. While food costs are not much lower, except for those who have garden plots in the small towns, rents are less. Secondly, the costs on the farm may be less than the 70 percent of Miss Orshansky's latest estimate of nonfarm costs.

The investigations conducted by our Joint Congressional Economic Committee some years ago on rural poverty, under the chairmanship of Senator John Sparkman, convinced me however that rural poverty is in fact far more widespread than urban. This is particularly true in the South among the Negroes of the plantation country and among the poor whites of the hills and mountains. Poverty is also widespread among the Mexican-Americans and Indians of the Southwest, as well as in mining and rural areas. It is indeed the poverty of life of so many of the rural and small-town folk which has caused enormous numbers to migrate to the cities in a desperate attempt to better themselves. Urban poverty is, therefore, in part a transfer of rural poverty. Poverty is greatest where population pressures are least.

During the quarter of a century from 1940 to 1966 the farm

population of the country decreased by no less than 19 million —from 30.5 to 11.6 million. While the population of the country was increasing from 132 to 196 million or by 48 percent, the total farm population was falling by over 60 percent. From forming 23 percent of the nation's people, the farm group had fallen to 5.8 percent. In fact, it can be said that the potential loss was more than this. For if the proportion that the farm population formed in 1940 of the total for the country had remained constant during this period, the total population on the farm would have risen to 45 million instead of falling to 12. The countryside, therefore, can be said to have lost a potential increase of 15 million as well as its absolute decrease of 19 million.

This migration of labor from the farm to the city has always gone on. But in the past it was at a much slower rate. While the total number on the farms did not decrease appreciably during the twenty years from 1920 to 1940 (the loss was only 1½ million), the relative number fell from 30 to 23 percent. What had happened during those years was that the farms lost the equivalent of their natural growth—no more. But the exodus from the farms became virtually a hemorrhage after 1940. First came the war and the absorption into the armed forces of millions of young men, many of whom did not return when the war was over. The higher earnings in urban industry also operated as a capillary attraction to draw farm people away to the cities and towns. Industrial wages and salaries were increasing while farm incomes were holding back. There were also impelling forces driving men off the soil. New fertilizers and machinery were helping workers to produce more. Combined with the inelastic nature of the demand for farm products, these developments actually served to displace labor. The productivity of labor per man hour increased approximately fourfold in the quarter century from 1940 to 1966, and if the increase in capital is considered along with that of labor, the increase in output for each composite unit of input was slightly over 50 percent. As the incomes of the people as a whole increased, they spent a smaller and smaller proportion of the additional dollars in food. This gradual transfer of relative purchasing power led to a consequent gradual transfer of labor and population. The number of individual farms fell from 6.3 million in 1940 to 3.2 million in 1967, while the average size of the farms more than doubled from 167 to 359 acres.

One farmer with the aid of more machinery could farm more acres, and with the aid of better seed, insecticides, etc., and more knowledge, he could raise more on each acre. The result of all this was such an unparalleled exodus that during the seventeen years from 1950 to 1966 inclusive, over 16 million people migrated from the farms. Since 4 million had similarly left in the five years from 1945 to 1949, this made a total migration for the 22 years of about 20 million. This has been the number that the cities, suburbs and country towns have been compelled to absorb. Most of those who have left have been relatively low-income people. They have largely been owners and tenants on small farms and their families, who have found it impossible to compete in an age that requires more machinery and capital. But in large numbers they have also been impoverished farm laborers, who were squeezed out first. The rural poor have therefore become a large part of the urban, small-town and small-city poor.

Furthermore, many of our coal mines have either given out or have been forced out of business by high costs and reduced demand. Structural unemployment and its derivative evil, poverty, has been created by these factors. Technology has also shifted productive methods while demand has altered. Coal mining, for example, no longer employs its three quarters of a million workers with a dependent population of between three and four million people, and decayed coal-mining villages dot the countryside of both the anthracite and bituminous fields. The replacement of much train travel and freight service by the automobile and truck, together with the fact that diesels can haul longer trains than steam locomotives, has also decreased the numbers of both train crews and railway shop employees. This has caused a wasting away of the railroad division points and shop towns. There has been a similar decline in the former logging towns around the Great Lakes and in the Northwest.

Many of those forced off the farm and out of the mines and woods have not gone to the far-off big cities, but instead to the nearby small towns and county seats. On the outskirts of these smaller communities you can see their shantytowns, or, farther down on the bystreets, their shacks and decayed housing. In either case, they and their children are in need— great need. The small towns that were once trading centers for the farms have now lost their markets and seem destined to furnish the major part of future migration to the cities.

Tucked away in one of Miss Orshansky's tables is an illuminating comparison of the degree of poverty in various sections of the country in 1966. This is in terms of the 6.1 million families who are in poverty, rather than the 30 million people. The percentages of poverty amongst families are of course less than among persons, which are raised by the high proportion of large families among the poor. But the regional comparisons are significant:

FAMILIES IN POVERTY

Region	Number in 000's	Percent
Northeast	1037	8.6
North Central	1259	9.2
South	2950	19.7
West	840	10.1
TOTAL	6086	12.4

Here it will be seen that over twice as many families were poor in the South as in the Northeast and many more proportionately than in the Midwest. This has led to a migration of the poor to the North and West. It has been largely the exodus of Southern Negroes and Appalachian whites that has burdened St. Louis, East St. Louis, Chicago, Detroit, Newark and New York.

The groups most vulnerable to poverty are the children (particularly those in large families), the aged, families headed by a woman, the families of the unemployed and those in low-paid occupations.

In 1966, there were 12.5 million children under the age of eighteen who lived in poverty. They comprised 18 percent of all the children in this age group and 42 percent of all the poor. This compared with 15 percent for the population as a whole and only 9.5 percent for adults of eighteen to fifty-four who were living in families. If those who lived alone were included, the percentage for adults would rise to between 10 and 11 percent. And if those who were missed by the census were included, the number and percentage in both groups—i.e., those under eighteen and those in the early years of the adult group—would increase still more.

It needs to be emphasized that children formed the largest single age group among the poor: namely, three-sevenths of the total of 30 million. Of these poor children, a total of 4.5 million, well over a third, were in families headed by a woman. No fewer than three out of every five children (61 percent) in such families were in fact poor. But it is also important to realize that there were no fewer than 8 million poor children who were in unbroken families with a male head of household.

The old people, sixty-five years and over, were the next largest age group among the poor. They numbered 5.4 mil-

lion, forming 18 percent of the total number of the poor, and
were divided evenly between those living alone and those in
a family group. About 55 percent of those who lived alone
were poor as compared with 20 percent of those in a family.

The children and the aged comprised, therefore, 18 of the 30
million people listed as poor, or 60 percent of the total. This
left 12 million, or 40 percent of the poor, who were between
the ages of eighteen and sixty-five and who were therefore
in the so-called "productive years." Of these, 2.4 million were
women struggling to support a family without the help of a
husband, and these had no less than 4½ million children to
support.

It is a sobering thought that there were in 1966 slightly over
20 million or over two-thirds of the ranks of the poor in the
three classes which most command the sympathies of the American people—children, the aged, and mothers with fatherless
children to support. Since our systems of public relief and
assistance aim to take care of the last two classes and a considerable fraction of the first, and since the payments from
these welfare sources are also included in the incomes received, a preliminary glimpse is given of the relative in-
adequacy of these aids and of the huge volume of poverty
that still persists among over 20 million people.

There was a residual of between 9 and 10 million of the
poor who were adults in the active years of life and in families
headed by men. At least one and a half to two million of these
were so handicapped by crippling diseases and accidents as
to be classed among the permanently and severely disabled.

This left around 8 million adults who were still in poverty.
There were, however, several million men and women among
these who were in the age group below 65 years but who were
judged "not to be in the labor force" and who were therefore
presumably out of work for the entire year. There were also an
additional 780,000 men and women below the age of sixty-five

who, though regarded as part of the working force, were unemployed for part or all of the year. To be conservative, we
can therefore estimate that unemployment was the chief proximate cause for the poverty of at least 3 million adults as well
as an unknown number of dependents.

The final group consisted of the million and a half men who
though employed steadily throughout the year did not earn
enough to support their dependents. This number would be
approximately doubled by including dependent wives. There
were also 4½ million children in these families, and Miss
Orshansky estimates that the total number of persons in these
families came to approximately 8 million or "one-third of the
poor who were not keeping house for themselves." * These
were families where the wages were so low that in spite of
continuous work by the husbands and fathers they could not
support their dependents on even a poverty level. These
totals were somewhat lower, however, than they had been
three years before, when there were 2 million heads of families who though they worked steadily did not earn enough to
support their families, which then included somewhere between 9 and 10 million people.

These low earnings were especially characteristic of farm
workers and unskilled labor. Thus in 1963 half of the Negro
farm laborers in the prime of life earned less than $975.
Among Negro farmers the average was still lower, namely
$945. The corresponding figure for white farm laborers in
the same age group was $2,020 or more than twice as much
as the Negro average, and for white farmers and managers or
tenants the mid-point was $2,945 or three times as much.
Among the so-called common laborers off the farm, the mid-
point of earnings for Negroes was $2,825 and for whites $4,095,

* Mollie Orshansky, *Who Was Poor in 1966,* Research and Statistics
Note No. 23, 1967, Department of Health, Education, and Welfare,
December 1967.

45 percent more than the median for Negroes. Among the women workers domestic service was, of course, the lowest-paid occupation. In 1966, 38 percent or three-eighths of the male laborers and their families were in poverty, as were 63 percent or five-eighths of the women working as domestics in private homes.

At least two other groupings among the poor need to be noted—groupings by race and by size of families.

There is a common belief that poverty is primarily confined to Negroes and to other nonwhites. This is emphatically not the case. Poverty is indeed much greater among these groups than it is among the whites, but since other groups than the native whites of European stock form only about 14 or 15 percent of the population, they comprise only a minority, although a significant number of the poor.*

Thus in 1963, although 49 percent of the nonwhites were in poverty as compared with 14½ percent of the whites (a ratio of more than three to one), they formed only 30 percent of the total number of the poor. Seventy percent of the poor were whites.

By 1966 the total number of Negroes and other nonwhites who were actually in poverty had diminished, but they nevertheless formed a slightly larger percentage of the poor, namely 34 instead of 30 percent.† This came about because the whites

---

* The nonwhites include, in addition to Negroes (who in 1966 were listed as numbering 21.5 million), Indians, Japanese, Chinese, Filipinos and others such as Malaysians, Polynesians, Eskimos, etc. The total of nonwhites other than Negroes numbered 1.6 million in 1960 and probably 1.9 million in 1966. This would come to a combined total of 23.4 million or 12 percent of the 1966 population. If the Mexican-American or Spanish-language minorities were also to be included, the total number would probably be increased by at least 2 percent, or by a total of about 4 million, to something over 27 million. The undercounting of these groups by the census would moreover not only raise their total but also their proportion to about 15 percent of the population.

† This would have been greater had the Mexican-Americans been included among the nonwhites.

had made a greater relative progress during the intervening three years, but approximately two-thirds of the poor were still whites. Poverty is therefore no respecter of races, but strikes the disadvantaged among all.

No greater mistake could indeed be made than to aim the campaign against poverty exclusively, or even predominantly, for the benefit of the Negro poor. The Negroes are indeed the most conspicuous among the poor. They are also the most militant and have suffered the most at the hands of white society. They must be helped. But they are also a decided minority of those who live in poverty. In New York City the Puerto Ricans, whether their color be dark or light, have felt neglected by the concentration of effort upon the Negroes. In the Southwest the Mexican-Americans are probably the most neglected among the poor. And it is important not to slight poor whites such as those from the Appalachians.

The poor whites are reluctant to complain and they are commonly more hesitant about applying either for welfare or for public housing. This is partly because of a fierce sense of independence and personal pride and partly because they do not want to admit that they are in the same economic plight as the Negroes. Thus in the District of Columbia, of the 30,000 families that in 1966 had an income of less than $3,000, there were 21,600 nonwhite to 8,460 white families, making the respective percentages 72 and 28. But while the whites formed two-sevenths of the poor families in 1966, only 4 percent of the mothers receiving aid for dependent children were white, and only 2 percent of those in public housing.* The whites simply did not apply.

When our Commission on Urban Problems in 1967 held hearings in eighteen widely distributed cities over the country, scores of the Negro poor appeared before us to complain

* See the articles by Michael Bernstein, "A Strange Dilemma in Our City," *Washington Daily News,* January 29 and 30, 1967.

about the conditions under which they lived and worked. Their complaints were well founded. But not a single white member of the poor appeared. And while the whites were not completely absent from the ranks of the city rioters in 1966 and 1967, and in the Poor People's March on Washington in 1968, they were relatively so.

But the failure of the whites to protest should not lead to their neglect. They are also in trouble and they should be sought out and helped. Unless they are, they will conclude, as multitudes have already done, that the housing and anti-poverty measures are not for them but are instead only for Negroes. They will therefore cherish a deep resentment against society and will dislike the Negroes more than ever. Instead of the poor feeling a basic solidarity with each other, as they should, they will break up into conflicting racist groups of blacks, Puerto Ricans, Mexican-Americans and native whites. All are likely to lose by this cleavage. And in the process, racial strife is likely to be increased rather than diminished.

As one would expect, poverty increases with the number of children in a family. This is shown very graphically for 1966 by Miss Orshansky:

Size of Families	Percentage Classed as Poor
1 child	9
2 children	10
3 children	13
4 children	18
5 children	28
6 or more children	42

Thus, the proportion of poor families among those with five children is three times as great as among the one-child families, while it was four to five times greater in families with six or more children. What Margaret Sanger observed over a half-century ago is most emphatically true today.

When women are forced to take up the tasks customarily assigned to men and compelled to bear the burden of family support, the proportion of the families in poverty sky-rockets. Whereas only 14 percent of the families headed by males were in poverty, no less than 50 percent, or a full half, of the families of which mothers were the heads were in need. The more children the mothers had to support, the worse off they were: among the families headed by a woman with six or more children, 86 percent were poor.

The case for birth control and family planning among the poor is therefore strengthened by these figures. When one disadvantage is piled on top of another, the suffering is compounded.

Poverty has many forms and many immediate causes. Low earnings are one factor and lack of education another. Unemployment, sickness and disability take their toll. Old age lowers earning power. Large families strain the family purse and help to plunge millions into poverty. Women are handicapped in comparison with men. The aged and single are plunged into far greater hardships than their brothers. The burdens of the mothers are even heavier. Husbands and lovers may desert and escape their responsibilities, but the mothers stay and must bear the double burden of bringing up the family and trying to earn a living. Those of dark skin are handicapped and have a poverty ratio over three times greater than that for whites.

Of course those who lack the will to work (except for the wealthy idlers) must live on the fringes of society, and they and their dependents suffer accordingly.

Those who combine two or more of these disadvantages become even more submerged. In the language of social workers, they are "multi-problemed." Negro children in large families without a male head and cared for by an ignorant mother are the most acutely handicapped. These handicaps cause poverty in many cases. In others they are also caused by poverty. Sometimes cause and effect are so intertwined that it becomes impossible to determine which came first.

To conclude, there are many causes of poverty and our most constructive social effort should be to reduce it to the lowest possible limit. We cannot plead that we lack the material means to make this effort, for in the fourth quarter of 1967 we had a gross national product of goods and services of $827 billion. This was an arithmetic average of over $4,100 a person or over $16,000 for a family of four. We can greatly reduce the numbers who are in poverty, if we only have the will to do so. Congress made such a pledge in 1965 with the Economic Opportunity Act. The question is whether we mean it. If we can spend $30 to $40 billion to put a man on the moon and then return him, is it beyond our power to end the grossest forms of poverty within our country?

I believe that this challenge is more important than that of space. It is more vital socially than the demands for a super- sonic airliner, or irrigation in the high mountains. It should take precedence over the depletion allowance on oil and gas or the exemption from taxation of much of capital gains. It is distressing to see so many in Congress, reflecting without doubt the prevailing opinion among their constituents, oppose the very idea of aid to the poor, and, if forced to concede on that point, seek to reduce this aid to the lowest possible limits. Only a greater sense of human brotherhood on the part of the comfortable can reverse this trend.

6 *The Reduction in Poverty*

In the previous chapter, we have shown the volume of poverty in 1966 and have analyzed its composition. It is important, however, to recognize that while the numbers and the proportion in poverty are still excessively high, they have been greatly reduced in recent years and that this progress has been relatively steady and consistent.

Thus, when Franklin Roosevelt declared in his second inaugural address in 1937 that he saw "one-third of a nation ill-housed, ill-clad, ill-nourished," he was understating rather than exaggerating the actual situation. For the true proportion was then much nearer three-eighths (37 percent). One-third would have amounted to 43 million, three-eighths to

48 million people. The actual number may indeed have been appreciably more than this. By 1947, according to the Census Bureau estimates, the poor numbered at least a quarter of the population. In 1959, their estimated number was set by the bureau at 39 million or 22 percent, and by 1962, the total had fallen to 37 million and the proportion to 20 percent.*
Then the 1963 study by the bureau and Miss Orshansky showed a total of 35 million and 19 percent. The corresponding figures for the next four years were as follows:

Year	Estimated Number in Poverty	Percentage of Population
1964	34.1 million	18.0
1965	32.6 million	17.1
1966	29.7 million	15.7
1967	25.8 million	13.0

Because of the unavoidable failure to reach some of the submerged elements in the population, the total for each year, as has been pointed out, should probably be increased by about 2 million, and the proportion by about 1 percentage point. But this does not appreciably affect the relative rate of decrease.

There can be no question but that we have made great gains. From having one-third to three-eighths of the population in poverty, we have in thirty years cut this proportion at least in half and have reduced the absolute numbers by over 15 million even though the population has increased by slightly over 70 million, or by nearly 60 percent. The number and proportion of substandard houses has also sharply declined.

These are great achievements and should provide real reassurance to those of us who are not ourselves poor, although they can only give cold comfort to those who are still among

* *Statistical Abstract 1967*, p. 338.

the poor and have not "made it." No one can of course predict whether or not this rate of improvement will continue. If we are granted peace and the absence of a shattering economic depression, such as we experienced in the 1930's, and provided that the same social policies are followed, we can have some reassurance that the proportions in poverty will continue to decline. Since the relative percentages were cut in half in the thirty years between 1936 and 1966, it would seem plausible that the percentage in poverty by the end of the century could be somewhere around 8 percent. With an estimated total population at that time of 300 million, this would give a total in poverty of 24 million. This is altogether too large a total to be contemplated with any equanimity. Our resolution should be strengthened rather than weakened by the progress we have made.

The great gains already made are the result of a variety of forces. Among those are: (1) increased productivity per man, caused by such factors as more capital per worker, and improvement in industrial technique, personal abilities, and training; (2) a decrease in the average amount of unemployment; (3) a consequent rise in real earnings and income; (4) an increased internal migration from lower- to higher-income areas; (5) an increased public concern over the status of the poor as evidenced in collective action.

The evidence for these gains is quite clear. The gross national product at current prices rose from $100 billion in 1940 to $807 billion by the end of 1967. In terms of dollars of constant purchasing power, the increase was from $246 to $669 billion, or an increase of 170 percent. The per capita increase from 1950 to 1966 was 40 percent. A more refined measurement is probably the total disposable personal income. In practice, this gives approximately the same relative results. For this increased from a total of $207 billion in 1950 to $557 billion at the end of 1967. This was an increase of

170 percent. In terms of dollars of constant purchasing power, the per capita increase in real income was from $1,646 to $2,294, or a gain of 40 percent.

Pursuing this theme still further, we find that the physical output per man-hour outside of agriculture increased by about 70 percent between 1947 and 1966. In agriculture, output per man-hour actually tripled in the same period of time.* A part of this increase was due to the fact that each employee now worked with a greater quantity of capital than before. After many years of inductive work, I concluded in 1947 that in manufacturing an increase of 1 percent in the quantity of capital for each unit of labor tended to increase output by around two-thirds of 1 percent. Interestingly enough, later statistical studies by others tend to support this conclusion.

The improvement in the educational levels of the population has been marked. Of every 1,000 students who in 1926 were in the fifth grade, only 33 percent subsequently graduated from high school and only 129 (13 percent) entered college. Of a similar group in 1959, 72 percent later graduated from high school and 40 percent entered college. I agree with my friend and former colleague Theodore Schultz that this has been a measurable factor in raising the productivity of labor.

This general increase in productivity has of course also operated to increase the average earnings of both the employees and the self-employed. The average weekly money earnings in manufacturing more than quadrupled from 1940 to 1966, and in retail trade approximately tripled. In terms of weekly real earnings, the increase in manufacturing over this quarter of a century amounted to a little over 90 percent and in retail trade to about 40 percent.†

Along with the increase in the payment for work went a decrease in the amount of unemployment. This was reduced

---

* *Ibid.*, p. 236.
† *Ibid.*, p. 238.

from an average of not far from 14 percent of the working force in 1940 to an official figure of 5.6 percent in 1960 and to around 4 percent for the last few years. In the winter and spring of 1967–68, the official index fell to as low as 3.5 percent. While these latter averages, as we have seen, seriously understate the actual amount of unemployment, there can be no doubt that there has been a real reduction in the relative amount.

Another ingredient in the gains that have been made has been the shift from areas with lower earnings to those with higher. During the ten years from 1950 to 1960, there were no fewer than 3 million whites who migrated from eighteen states and 1.66 million nonwhites who left the Southern states. A primary reason for the migration was the higher level of earnings in the states into which they went. While a considerable percentage failed to catch on in their new environment, it can be presumed that a majority did. For if they had not, the flow would not have continued. In addition, the movement from farms to cities inside the states also raised the level of earnings. We have seen this in Illinois as families from southern Illinois have moved into the Chicago area and other urban centers, and this has also gone on within virtually every other state. There were indeed approximately 30 million people in 1960 who were living in a different county from that in which they had lived five years before.

A final factor in the improvement has been the increase in so-called free income. Cash transfers to those with relatively low income come primarily through the medium of public assistance and social insurance. To this should be added the provision of additional services to the lower-income groups, either without cost or at less than cost. These services take the form of added education, medical and hospital care, recreation and personal counseling and protection. I have already given some figures on the extension of education from

1926 to 1966. Public expenditures for elementary and secondary education almost quadrupled from $5.8 billion to $21.3 billion from 1950 to 1964. The current contributions to higher education from both public and private sources rose from $250 million in 1940 to slightly over $5 billion in 1964. Public funds for outdoor recreation more than doubled. Public expenditures on health increased from less than a billion dollars in 1940 to nearly $11 billion in 1966. Private philanthropy increased its recorded aid from less than $100 million in 1940 to $850 million in 1966. Private contributions for the construction of medical facilities rose from only $30 million in 1940 to over $1.3 billion in 1966. Private contributions to the so-called character-building institutions also increased. The various local United Fund campaigns raised $86 million in 1940 and $625 million in 1966. Charitable foundations of appreciable size numbered in 1964–65 nearly 7,000, had $20 billion in assets and spent $1.2 billion. Total contributions to religious bodies amounted to $3.2 billion in 1965, of which $2.6 billion went for congregational expenses and slightly less than $600 million for benevolences.

For obvious reasons, it is difficult to compute the total amounts spent for all these services; a rough estimate of $40 billion a year would not be unreasonable.

A considerable portion of these services has seeped down to the lowest quarter or third of the population, but just how much can probably never be measured. It is, however, a significant amount and it has increased markedly in the last quarter of a century.

Yet, despite all our material progress and the reduction in the number of the poor, uncertainty and discontent are more widespread now than they were twenty years ago when we emerged victorious from a great world struggle. Riots have swept most of our cities. Our racial minorities show greater bitterness than ever before. Resentment among the poor has risen. Guerrilla warfare seems to have started in many places.

All this has in turn puzzled and embittered members of the economically comfortable and dominant social classes. If economic conditions are getting better, how is it that social conditions are growing worse? How is it that hatred and discontent are increasing as the numbers of the poor are shrinking?

The answers to these questions differ widely. While millions have risen, those who have remained in the bottom 30 million have not really improved their personal situations. They are still in poverty, and they are still ill-housed. Because of their poverty and frequently because of their color, they tend to be looked down upon by an affluent society and treated as pariahs and failures. They are therefore largely isolated from the rest of society. They are, in Michael Harrington's expressive term, "the other America," or, in the eyes of the upper layers of society, the invisible poor. Nobody likes such treatment. All who have suffered from it naturally resent it. They want to be accepted as equal members of the community and not dismissed as a despised lower sediment.

A large proportion of the poor families have lived in this condition for years and usually for generations, and these have largely lost hope. They live, as their parents and grandparents lived, in deprivation and need. It has always been that way with them. They believe that is the way it will always be. And they see no greater hope for their children or indeed their children's children. Whether they come from the rural or the urban poor, poverty is a hereditary disease, partly environmental, but probably also partly innate, caused by deep biological and physical handicaps. But an ordinary child born to poor parents in an urban slum bears other heavy hardships in the lack of adequate food, education, cultural influences and all the crushing negative forces. Poverty therefore perpetuates itself from generation to generation. The effect becomes itself the most important cause. Millions remain poor and are doomed to be so because that is what their fathers and mothers were.

At the same time, by television and observation, they are aware of the increased affluence of the middle and upper economic classes. In an imperfect and sometimes exaggerated manner, they see the concentration of wealth, income and power among the topmost groups in our society. They do not know the precise details—that the bottom fifth of the families, to which they belong, received in 1965 only 4 to 5 percent of the national income, whereas the top fifth received 41 to 45 percent and the top 5 percent received 15 percent.* But they know that while they receive little, others receive much. And in the advertisements on television, which now go into nearly every home, they see how the affluent are supposed to live, how they eat, how they are clothed, and how they can take expensive trips and ride around in expensive automobiles. If they see all this and feel little hope that they can rise, is it any wonder that they feel resentful and frustrated and that they strike out at a system that seems to condemn them to a permanent life of deprivation and inferiority, while the social surplus belongs to others?

Nor is their resentment lessened by the fact that millions of their former associates in poverty have improved their status and have risen out of the ranks of the poor. They haven't. They are left behind. And as other incomes rise, the distance between the average family and the poor widens rather than narrows. Further, those who were formerly poor but who are now lower middle class, take a great deal of personal credit for their own good fortune and tend to look down upon and to separate themselves from their former companions in misery. This in turn naturally increases the resentment and

* *Statistical Abstract 1967*, pp. 333–36.

frustration of those at the bottom. And this feeling is particularly acute among youth.

All this is heightened and intensified by the factor of race. The 22 million Negroes are necessarily aware of the historic wrongs that the white race has committed against their ancestors. The whites want to forget all this. But the Negroes cannot and don't want to do so. Most Negroes have themselves felt manifold slights and injuries at the hands of whites. It is but natural that they should have deep, pent-up hatreds and frustrations. In the South, they were scattered over the countryside with the whites in full possession of the law and the instruments of violence. The Negroes were therefore afraid to rebel and lacked the means to do so. They were compelled to suffer in silence. In coming to the Northern cities, they carried with them their resentments and pent-up anger. Here they experienced new rebuffs. But they were now together and could not only communicate but act together. They had the vote and possessed political power. Public opinion was opposed to police or individual brutality. As a result, the city Negroes lost many of their fears and were far more ready to explode.

Even those who had progressed felt that progress should be faster. The civil rights legislation of 1964 and 1965 had aroused their hopes but had not given them appreciable immediate benefits. It was natural therefore that the inner volcanic fires should erupt as individual and specific grievances occurred. Here the unsuccessful and the poor were often joined and led by those who apparently had gained most.

This should not surprise the student of history. The French Revolution was most intense in those sections of France where the peasantry and the people had made the greatest progress. The monarchy and the old order was strongest in those sections of France, such as Brittany and La Vendée, where the material progress had been least.

But now a second interesting paradox has developed. While discontent with the social order has multiplied, it has been a formless and relatively incoherent discontent. The old faiths of a half century ago are being repudiated along with the institutions of today. Formerly, many of the warm-hearted and most generous people who dissented from a fatalistic acceptance of poverty were advocates of some form of socialism. They believed that the only effective cure for poverty was to socialize the means of production and distribution so that all would be paid a living wage and at the same time be protected against the risks of accidents, sickness, unemployment, and old age.

Today this collectivist philosophy is far less popular in the United States. People correctly believe that it would be less efficient because the individual incentive for effort would be reduced. They also fear that the creation of an all-powerful state would probably lead to coercive terrors like those practiced by Nazi Germany and Communist Russia. Men have certainly not shown themselves fit to exercise absolute power. The six million Jews gassed to death by the Nazis and the thirty million Russians worked and frozen to death in the Communist labor camps should forever warn us away from any such monolithic alternatives. The Chinese experiences of the 1950's and the recent past reinforce these fears, while in Great Britain the public ownership of coal, steel and transport has not improved either efficiency or productivity as its advocates in the British Labour Party had promised.

The reforms that are necessary in this country will therefore be conducted under the basic system of private and, we hope, competitive enterprise. A wider distribution of property and power is highly desirable. But we should not throw the baby out with the bath water. Nor should we embrace a formless nihilism which scorns order and the patient attack upon concrete problems.

7 Public Efforts to Reduce Poverty

Operating cautiously, with social concern but within the private enterprise system, the country decided during the New Deal days of the thirties to try to protect people from some of the extreme hardships created within modern society. This was primarily carried through by the Social Security Act of 1935 and by its later amendments and extensions.* Two lines of defense against poverty were set up. The first was an outer system of social insurance financed by contributions from employers and employees. The inner line of defense was a limited system of public assistance or welfare for those in need, which was to be financed out of taxes by the state and national governments.

* Also of course by the Wages and Hours Act of 1938.

The insurance system in turn consisted of two parts, one for unemployment and one for old age. The former was designed to provide benefits for a limited period of time to those who had lost their jobs through no fault of their own and who, although able and seeking to work, were unable to find suitable employment. Only the employers made a direct contribution to the unemployment insurance funds—on the very questionable assumption that insurance against unemployment should be on a principle similar to that of compensation for industrial accidents; thus, the employers were made solely liable, on the ground that they were in the best position to reduce or prevent the flaws involved.

The insurance system for old age, which came to be termed "social security," was designed to provide automatic benefits based primarily on past earnings for those who had reached the age of sixty-five or over and who were employed in the covered occupations. It was to be jointly and equally financed by employers and employed.

Behind these outer lines designed to help protect millions from two of the hazards of modern life, a second and inner line was partially erected. This was a system of public assistance for some of those in need, which was to be jointly financed out of taxes by the federal and state governments but was to be directly administered by the latter.

There were three categories of the needy who were originally included under the assistance program: (1) the aged, who, despite social security, were still in need and who were initially the most important, (2) families with dependent children who were left with only one parent as a result of death, divorce, or desertion; originally thought to be a less important category, and (3) the blind, who made an especial appeal to the sympathy of the nation.

There were two significant qualifications that prevailed from the very beginning. The first was that such federal aid was not given to all the needy but merely to the categories described above. Indeed, at the same time (1935) that the social insurance and assistance plan was enacted, general relief programs were eliminated. The government continued to provide a considerable volume of work for adults through the WPA and for youths through the CCC, but it cut off federal funds for general relief. This was left completely to the states. Secondly, no national minimum standards for assistance were laid down. These were to be determined by the states.

This system of public assistance was primarily distinguished from insurance benefits in that it was not a legal right but merely a gratuity, which could be altered by decision of the state. Insurance benefits, on the other hand, were a right of the recipient and could not be denied by administrative fiat, for they were based in some ratio upon past earnings, whereas assistance grants were based upon the relative need of the recipient.

As the years passed by, the coverage of the insurance systems began to be broadened. Old-age security was widened to include benefits for widows and surviving children of the insured. Then the self-employed were brought into the ranks of those covered and were assessed at a rate of 1½ times that for employees. In the middle fifties, those over the age of fifty who were severely disabled were added to the insurance system. Later the entrance age for benefits to this group was reduced. In keeping with the parallel practice for the aged, public assistance was also provided for those severely disabled who were in need, either because of ineligibility for insurance benefits or because these benefits were inadequate. Combined with such public assistance has been a federal-state program for vocational rehabilitation conducted under the efficient direction of Miss Mary Switzer.

During the recessions of the late fifties and of 1960–61, the period of benefits under unemployment compensation was extended with federal aid, and finally in 1962, those who had exhausted their claims to unemployment benefits and were in need were made eligible for federal assistance if a state would meet half the cost. Only twenty-two states however have accepted this. In 1965 the insurance system was also greatly expanded by providing coverage for given amounts of hospital and nursing-home care for those over the age of sixty-five and, on a voluntary basis, for the costs of medical care as well. The parallel program of medical assistance was greatly extended from the previous vendor payments to doctors and hospitals serving the aged who were on relief to a broader group of the "medically indigent."

Under this new system of "medicaid," those eligible for medical and hospital payments were not limited to those included under the various relief categories, but were instead extended to the "medically indigent" of all ages, whether or not they were under federally-assisted categories. The definition of the "medically indigent" was, moreover, intended to cover not only the poor and "abject poor" but also those on the fringes of poverty and sections of the middle class as well. And if a state such as New York wished to extend this protection to the lower layers of the middle class, it was allowed to do so under the 1965 terms of Title XIX.*

It is crucial to recognize that as far as cash payments are concerned, the federal-state assistance system for the needy is not general in its nature but is limited to the specific categories that have been mentioned. It has grown gradually by accretion. It does not apply, therefore, to such groups as those in need under the age of sixty-five who are not blind or otherwise severely disabled, nor to those in the twenty-eight states

---

* The total amount of medical aid given under the Kerr-Mills Act and Title XIX of the Social Security Act of 1966 amounted in 1966 to just under $2 billion. It was running at the rate of $3 billion a year in September 1967. *Social Security Bulletin*, January 1968, p. 275.

that have not taken advantage of the assistance provisions for the long-time unemployed.

Phrased more directly, no federal aid in the form of cash is granted for the needy in the active years of life (under sixty-five) who have moved into the cities from un-covered occupations on the farms and the small towns. These folks are ineligible for unemployment compensation payments as well as for federal aid on assistance payments unless special arrangements are made by the states. Similarly, while most of the costs of medical aid are now assumed for those over sixty-five by the insurance features of medicare, and for the medically indigent both above and below this age by medicaid, there are no federal cash benefits to meet the running expenses of a family impoverished by illness.* But health insurance laws in four states provided payments in 1966 of $482 million, while private insurance paid out $1,135 million and sick leave a total of $1.96 billions. In all a total of approximately $3.6 billion was provided under various forms of protection against lost income from sickness. Forty percent of this, however, was in the form of sick leave for government employees. Since the total income lost from sickness is estimated at $12.2 billion, the proportion thus made good amounted to approximately 29 percent.

Social insurance or security benefits in 1966 were paid to just under 26 million persons and amounted to $31.5 billion. The distribution of this total by categories, exclusive of veterans' pensions and public assistance, was approximately as follows: †

---

* See an article in the *Social Security Bulletin*, January 1968, pp. 3–14, "Income Loss Protection Against Illness, 1948–60," by Alfred M. Skolnilz.
† *Social Security Bulletin*, May 1967; *ibid.*, April 1967, p. 29.

Form of Benefits	Cash Benefits in billions, 1966	Number Receiving Benefits in Dec. 1966, in millions
1. Old-age, disability and health insurance ("social security")	$20.8	20.8
2. Railway retirement	1.2	.9
3. Public employees' retirement	5.2	—
4. Lump-sum benefits	.3	—
5. Unemployment benefits and training allowances	2.1	1.0
6. Disability	.5	2.0
7. Workman's compensation	1.3	—
TOTALS	$31.4	24.7

The overwhelming portion of these benefits, nearly $28 billion, came from insurance funds to which the workers were joint and equal contributors. To this degree the payments made to beneficiaries were not a net addition to the total income of the employed workers but were rather a redistribution of those incomes. They permitted however a better distribution of the losses from illness or old age and greatly diminished the number who were plunged into poverty because of loss of earning power.*

The question of who ultimately pays the half of the benefits advanced by the employers is hotly disputed. It seems probable that a considerable portion of it is shifted back-

* We do not have the total number of public employees in receipt of benefits. There were approximately 900,000 receiving such benefits from the federal civil service. These are included in the totals. There are many more in the state, county and municipal systems. During 1967, the total sums paid out for all benefits covered in the above table amounted to $37.4 billion. The increase was largely caused by "medicare."

wards to the employees in the form of potential wage increases that are foregone, while some is shifted forward to
the consumers in the form of higher prices. But a portion,
and no one can say how much, may come out of profits. This
would be especially true in the cases of monopoly, near
monopoly, and highly imperfect competition. This general
system of social insurance has probably therefore had some
influence in lessening the inequality in the distribution of incomes. Even where the ultimate costs were borne by the employed and by the consumers, a more even distribution of income was effected, which reduced the numbers forced into
poverty. This follows from the familiar principle of insurance
whereby less hardship is created for the many, who make
slight contributions, than the few who must face catastrophic
losses would suffer without insurance.

Veterans' benefits are, however, paid for out of federal
revenues rather than from contributions by employer and employed. They rose from $2.8 billion in 1955 to $3.4 billion in
1960 and then to $4.34 billion in 1966. This 57 percent in-
crease was of course far greater than the increase in the cost
of living. While a considerable share of these benefits went to
those in the middle-income brackets, a portion also went to
those who were hard pressed. Since the federal tax structure,
despite its many faults, is still arithmetically progressive in
nature, this has provided some redistribution of income.*

The relief and welfare payments are also a very important
factor in increasing the actual incomes of the poor. These payments rose from $2.4 billion in 1950 to $3.4 billion in 1960 and
to $4.3 billion in 1966. This increase of 2.5 billions of dollars in

* Without social security, 59 percent of the families receiving it would
have been "poor." With it, 31 percent were. Without public assistance,
81 percent now receiving it would have been poor. With it, 67 percent
were.

NUMBER OF PUBLIC ASSISTANCE RECIPIENTS AND
AMOUNTS RECEIVED BY CATEGORIES IN 1966 *

Type of Assistance	Number of Recipients (in thousands)	Amount of Assistance (in millions)	Average Monthly Payment
1. Old-age	2,073	$1,634	$68
2. Blind	84	87	$87
3. Permanently and totally disabled	588	487	$75
4. Families with dependent children			
(a) families	1,127		$150
(b) children	3,526		
(c) total recipients	4,666	1,865	$36
5. General (not federally aided)	663	264	$36
TOTALS	8,074	$4,337	

* *Social Security Bulletin*, September 1967, p. 40.

seventeen years was a decided addition to the real income of some of the neediest sections of the population.

The general scope of the public assistance and welfare programs can be seen by the totals by categories for 1966 shown in the table above.

By November 1967, however, the number receiving assistance had increased by about 600,000, or to a total of 8.76 million.† The increase was overwhelmingly in the category of aid to dependent children, where the numbers rose from 4.7 to 5.2 million. The number of children helped increased by 400,000, from 3.5 to 3.9 million.‡ The number aided among the aged and blind remained virtually constant, but there were increases of 50 and 100 thousand respectively among the disabled and those on general relief. Approximately 4⅓ percent

† *Social Security Bulletin*, January 1968, p. 43.
‡ By February 1968 the number of children had further increased to 4.1 million and the total number on assistance to 9.1 million.

of the total population and 11.2 percent of the children under eighteen had received assistance.

As has been stated, these grants are theoretically not given as a legal right but rather as a gratuity on the basis of individual need. Although half a century ago we depended primarily on private charity, with governmental assistance serving in a merely supplementary role, today the roles are reversed; it is the government that now assumes the major responsibility, and private charity is merely supplementary. But need has to be determined by investigators, who go into the requirements and resources of the applicants, whereas the insurance benefits are based on past employment and earnings and do not require inquiry into the personal needs and resources of those who apply.

The two largest categories of assistance are those for old age and for families with dependent children. In November 1967 these included a total of 7.3 million recipients, or about 84 percent of the total. The number receiving old-age assistance has not increased within recent years but has remained constant at approximately 2.1 million. This has been largely owing to the greatly increased number of the aged who receive social security or insurance benefits, and to the more liberal benefits themselves. Thus the number of retired workers rose from 3.3 million in 1955 to 7.1 million in 1960 and to 11.7 million in 1966, while the number of dependent spouses who also received benefits rose from a little under a half million in 1955 to something over a million and a half in 1966.

It had been expected that these increases, together with the greater affluence of the population, would reduce not only the proportions but also the absolute number of those on old-age assistance. This has not yet occurred, and perhaps the most that can be said is that the extension of benefits and other factors have prevented the number from increasing. It is hoped that as these tendencies continue, the total number will also decrease.

There has been, on the other hand, a decided increase in the number of persons receiving aid for dependent children. This total rose from 3.6 million in 1961 to 5.2 million in November 1967 and to 5.5 million in February 1965. This increase of 1.9 million amounted to slightly over 50 percent, and it occurred when the absolute numbers of the poor were decreasing fairly rapidly and when the average family income was rising appreciably. Critics of the welfare program have cited these facts as proof that many people are relying more and more upon the government rather than their own efforts, and that some women are having additional illegitimate children because of the fact that their maintenance is partially assured. These beliefs played a part in causing Congress in 1967 to tighten the eligibility rules for this type of assistance.

Although this charge may be in part true, the statistics do not prove it. In the first place, the average number of children per dependent family only rose from 3.0 in 1961 to 3.07 in February 1968. This is a hardly noticeable increase of 2 percent, which could well be accounted for by other factors. Secondly, the greater total number of families receiving assistance was probably a result of the increased movement of the poorer families from the rural areas to the cities, and to a greater awareness by women among the poor of their legal rights and opportunities. Another factor, of course, was the fact that since general relief to families headed by males was extremely scanty, and unemployment compensation was largely closed to the new migrants, increased pressure was placed on men to desert their families in order that they might be at least partially cared for.

Tables 1 and 2 (pages 164–167) show not only the numbers but also the proportions of the aged and the children who received these two forms of assistance, for the country as a whole and also for states and geographic districts. It is believed that the percentage and regional comparisons are made here for the first time. It should be noted that while the

TABLE 1

NUMBER AND PERCENTAGES OF THOSE 65 AND OVER IN RECEIPT
OF OLD-AGE ASSISTANCE—AUGUST 1967 *

State and Region	(1) Number 65 and over—1966 (in thousands)	(2) Number receiving old-age assistance— Aug. 1967 (in thousands)	(3) Percentage of aged receiving assistance $(3) = (2) \div (1)$
New England	1,200	79.6	6.7
Maine	111	10.2	9.2
New Hampshire	73	4.2	5.8
Vermont	44	4.2	9.5
Massachusetts	607	49.3	8.1
Rhode Island	96	4.5	4.7
Connecticut	269	7.2	2.7
Middle Atlantic	3,731	128.3	3.4
New York	1,893	70.5	3.7
New Jersey	640	13.8	2.2
Pennsylvania	1,198	44.0	3.7
East North Central	3,645	182.4	5.0
Ohio	957	67.3	7.0
Indiana	471	19.4	4.1
Illinois	1,059	38.8	3.7
Michigan	713	39.8	5.6
Wisconsin	445	17.1	3.8
West North Central	1,837	175.4	9.6
Minnesota	391	25.9	6.6
Iowa	345	24.4	7.1
Missouri	529	88.8	16.8
North Dakota	62	4.4	7.1
South Dakota	78	5.6	7.2
Nebraska	175	8.9	5.1
Kansas	257	17.4	6.8
South Atlantic	2,488	270.1	11.3
Delaware	40	1.8	4.5
Maryland	261	7.8	3.0

* *Social Security Bulletin,* December 1967, Table M-24, p. 53; *Statistical Abstract of the United States* 1967, Table no. 20A, p. 25.

State and Region	(1) Number 65 and over—1966 (in thousands)	(2) Number receiving old-age assistance— Aug. 1967 (in thousands)	(3) Percentage of aged receiving assistance (3) = (2) ÷ (1)
South Atlantic (Cont.)			
District of Columbia	73	2.2	3.0
Virginia	326	11.2	3.4
West Virginia	183	11.8	6.4
North Carolina	362	39.5	10.9
South Carolina	172	22.0	12.8
Georgia	327	95.3	29.1
Florida	743	78.5	10.6
East South Central	*1,148*	*297.7*	*25.9*
Kentucky	314	60.7	19.3
Tennessee	342	47.7	13.9
Alabama	289	114.0	39.4
Mississippi	204	75.3	36.9
West South Central	*1,632*	*500.4*	*30.7*
Arkansas	211	64.8	30.7
Louisiana	270	125.0	46.3
Oklahoma	272	80.6	29.6
Texas	878	230.0	26.2
Mountain	*611*	*80.0*	*13.1*
Idaho	64	3.8	5.9
Montana	67	3.9	5.8
Wyoming	29	2.0	6.9
Colorado	172	40.8	23.7
New Mexico	62	9.6	15.5
Arizona	123	12.9	10.9
Utah	70	4.5	6.4
Nevada	24	2.5	10.4
Pacific	*2,163*	*328.8*	*15.2*
Washington	301	26.3	8.7
Oregon	206	9.3	4.5
California	1,611	290.0	18.0
Alaska	7	1.4	20.0
Hawaii	38	1.8	4.7
Total United States	*18,457*	*2,068.0*	*11.2*

TABLE 2

State and Region	(1) Number of children under 18 (1966) (in thousands)	(2) Number receiving aid to dependent children (in thousands)	(3) Percentage of children receiving such aid (3) = (2) ÷ (1)
New England	3,886	188.6	4.9
Maine	357	15.4	4.3
New Hampshire	241	4.2	1.7
Vermont	149	5.6	3.8
Massachusetts	1,844	98.8	5.4
Rhode Island	300	21.3	7.1
Connecticut	996	43.3	4.3
Middle Atlantic	12,281	857.0	7.0
New York	6,025	549.0	9.1
New Jersey	2,342	105.0	4.5
Pennsylvania	3,913	203.0	5.2
East North Central	14,143	571.0	4.0
Ohio	3,779	154.0	4.1
Indiana	1,818	38.1	2.1
Illinois	3,802	206.0	5.4
Michigan	3,190	130.0	4.1
Wisconsin	1,555	42.9	2.8
West North Central	5,746	226.5	3.9
Minnesota	1,360	44.2	3.3
Iowa	986	33.4	3.4
Missouri	1,554	84.8	5.5
North Dakota	252	7.1	2.8
South Dakota	265	10.1	3.8
Nebraska	529	16.9	3.2
Kansas	800	30.0	3.8
South Atlantic	11,318	514.2	4.8
Delaware	195	11.7	6.0
Maryland	1,344	79.4	6.0
District of Columbia	276	19.9	7.2

State and Region	(1) Number of children under 18 (1966) (in thousands)	(2) Number receiving aid to dependent children (in thousands)	(3) Percentage of children receiving such aid (3) = (2) ÷ (1)
South Atlantic (Cont.)			
Virginia	1,643	42.8	2.6
West Virginia	636	67.8	10.7
North Carolina	1,856	78.9	4.3
South Carolina	1,020	21.0	2.1
Georgia	1,703	76.7	4.5
Florida	2,045	116.0	5.7
East South Central	*4,833*	*281.9*	*5.8*
Kentucky	1,167	75.1	6.4
Tennessee	1,390	71.7	5.2
Alabama	1,336	57.8	4.3
Mississippi	940	77.3	8.2
West South Central	*7,110*	*271.6*	*3.8*
Arkansas	714	28.4	4.0
Louisiana	1,454	92.4	6.4
Oklahoma	843	66.3	7.9
Texas	4,099	84.5	2.1
Mountain	*3,094*	*146.0*	*4.7*
Montana	271	7.4	2.7
Idaho	268	8.4	3.1
Wyoming	126	3.3	2.6
Colorado	739	41.2	5.6
New Mexico	446	28.2	6.3
Arizona	646	33.1	5.1
Utah	428	18.7	4.4
Nevada	170	5.7	3.4
Pacific	*8,853*	*642.4*	*7.3*
Washington	1,062	43.6	4.1
Oregon	678	26.9	4.0
California	6,708	554.0	8.3
Alaska	119	3.9	3.3
Hawaii	286	14.0	4.9
Total United States	71,265	3,699.2	5.2

numbers who received assistance are shown as of August and September of 1967, population statistics for that year were not available, so the Census Bureau estimates for the preceding year of 1966 are used. Since the average population growth in that year did not appreciably exceed one percent, any absolute or relative error would be minor.

As Table 1 shows, the proportion of the aged who received assistance amounted to 11.2 percent for the country as a whole, or to about one-ninth of all those of sixty-five years and over. While the 5.1 million in the assisted families with dependent children (including mothers) were approximately 2½ times as numerous as the assisted aged, they were only 2.6 percent of the total population. The number of children who were thus assisted increased by over a million from 2.75 million in 1961 to 3.8 million in September 1967. They formed in the latter month 5.4 percent of the 70.7 million children in the country who were under eighteen during the preceding year. This was at an average of about one child out of every eighteen. They were 4.1 million in February of 1968 and between 5.6 and 5.7 percent of those under eighteen.

Such were the general averages for the country as a whole.*
There were, however, thirteen states where the aged who were assisted formed less than 5 percent of the total number of the aged. These were Rhode Island, Connecticut, New York, New Jersey, Pennsylvania, Indiana, Illinois, Wisconsin, Delaware, Maryland, the District of Columbia, Virginia, Oregon and Hawaii. At the other extreme there were thirteen states where the proportion of the aged receiving assistance was more than

---

* In Puerto Rico there were 24.1 thousand of the aged who received assistance in September 1967 and the extraordinary number of 180,000 in families with dependent children. This was about 6½ percent of the total population. A corresponding figure for all of the states would have been 13 instead of 5.1 million. The average monthly benefit for the aged was $8.70, and for the members of the aided families only $4.95.

15 percent. These were Missouri, Georgia, Kentucky, Alabama, Mississippi, Arkansas, Louisiana, Oklahoma, Texas, Colorado, New Mexico, California and Alaska. In Louisiana no less than 46 percent of the aged, or nearly one-half, received old age assistance, while the ratios were also extraordinarily high in Alabama, Mississippi, Arkansas and Oklahoma. In the first two states the ratios were between 35 and 40 percent and in the latter two they grazed 30 percent.

The following general conclusions can probably be drawn from these statistics on the relative number of the aged receiving assistance by states and regions: (1) that the proportions were particularly low in the original Atlantic Coast states of the Union ranging from Maine to Virginia, and (2) that the ratios were especially high in the South Central states where poverty is great and where the early programs of the late Huey P. Long have had a profound effect. The doctrines of Dr. Francis Townsend and the political influence of the aged helped in turn to raise the percentages in California, Colorado and Florida, where the numbers of the retired aged are high, and in certain other states as well. On the whole it can be said that the proportion of the aged who are aided increases as one moves south and west.

In the case of aid to dependent children, there was also a variance between the states from the countrywide average of 5.4 percent. This, however, was not as great as in the case of the aged. Statistics of these proportions by states and regions are shown in Table 2. Thus the proportion of children under eighteen who were being aided under the assistance program varied from a low of 1.7 percent in New Hampshire to a high of 10.7 percent in the hard-pressed state of West Virginia. Here, however, the maximum percentage was only six times the minimum, whereas in the case of the aged the percentage in the state with the highest ratio (Louisiana with 46.3 percent) was twenty-one times that of the state with the lowest

(New Jersey with 2.2 percent). It will be noted that the regional differences in the proportions aided are also much less in the case of the children than of the aged. Thus, for the children virtually all of the regions were within a variance of one-third from the countrywide average of 5.4 percent, whereas for the aged, two regions—the Middle Atlantic and the East North Central—had proportions that were from one-third to one-half the countrywide average of 11.2 percent, and two more regions where the percentage was from two to three times the national average.

It is also noticeable that many of the Southern states with extremely high percentages of the aged on assistance tended, on the contrary, to provide grants to less than the country-wide proportion for the young. Thus, Alabama, which provided on a percentage basis for three and a half times the national average for the aged, took care of only 80 percent of the national average for the children. The difference in Arkansas, Texas and Georgia was almost equally great. On the other hand, New York, which had a relatively low percentage of the aged receiving assistance amounting to only about one-third the national proportion, took care of a relatively high proportion of the children, i.e., 9.1 percent. California was an exception to the general rule that the proportion of the children aided varied in some inverse order to the proportion of the aged assisted, for there the proportions of the children and of the aged receiving assistance were each about one-half more than the respective national averages.

Undoubtedly, one cause of the high ratios in New York and California was the migration of low-income families into those states, combined with a greater degree of leniency in applying standards of eligibility. Possibly also the scale of assistance, particularly in New York, may have operated as a magnet to attract these unfortunates. Whatever the reason, to have one child out of every eleven, as in New York, or one out of twelve, as in California, living in a broken home without a male head is, to say the least, highly regrettable. These facts have caused the less understanding to try to impose ceilings on the proportions that could be aided.

The third most important group are those on general relief. As we have repeatedly pointed out, these people do not receive any federal aid, and in their case the state and local governments must bear the full cost of such aid as is given. The number who are thus aided has not increased but rather decreased in the last six years from a total of 1,069,000 in 1961 to 729,000 in September 1967. This was .7 percent of the 107 million between the ages of eighteen and sixty-four in 1966. In general, most states have been extremely niggardly in dealing with this group. In ten broadly distributed states, for example, no general relief at all was given in 1967. These were Florida, Idaho, Hawaii, Indiana, Kentucky, Nebraska, Ohio, Oklahoma, Texas and Vermont. In nine more states only a nominal number, less than a thousand, were aided. These were Alabama, Alaska, Arkansas, Nevada, New Mexico, North Dakota, Ohio, Oklahoma and Wyoming. There were four more states where the number thus helped ranged only between one and two thousand. There are in fact only a handful of states that have made any serious attempt to help these unfortunates who now fall between the specific categories of relief. New York is at the head of this list with 162,-000. Then comes Ohio with 75,000, Michigan with 62,000, California with 54,000, Illinois with 52,000, and finally New Jersey and Pennsylvania with 37,000 each. The 479,000 who were thus aided by these seven states were approximately two-thirds of the entire number in the country as a whole or 1.6 percent of those from eighteen to sixty-four.

But of course the amounts paid to those receiving aid are just as important, if not more so, than the numbers aided. As we mentioned earlier, the federal government did not fix any national or regional standard to be observed, but instead allowed each state to determine its own. The minimum subsistence levels that the states theoretically fixed were in general below the spartan levels set by Miss Orshansky as the upper limit for poverty. Thus in 1963 there were no less than fourteen states where the official state minimum for an aged woman pensioner was less than $90 a month, or $1,080 a year.* In addition there were twenty-one more states where the monthly minimum was between $90 and $109, or between $1,080 and $1,308 a year.† The first group were markedly below the poverty standard, while the second group were also below it. Four years later, in 1967, there were, however, only seven states where the standards were below $90 a month and seventeen between that figure and $109 a month.

The minimum standards of subsistence fixed by nine states in 1965 for a mother and three dependent children were less than $165 a month, or $2,000 a year,‡ while in thirteen more states the minimum standard fell between that figure and $194 a month, or $2,325 a year.§ The standard for the first group was close to that for "abject poverty" while that for the latter was still markedly below the national poverty level. There was an improvement in the published standards during the next two years, but just how much is not precisely known since the Social Rehabilitation Service now makes its compu-

---

* These were West Virginia, South Carolina, Tennessee, Georgia, Texas, Arkansas, Maryland, Kentucky, Illinois, the District of Columbia, Kansas, New Hampshire, Missouri and Rhode Island.
† These states were Mississippi, Maine, North Carolina, Iowa, Minnesota, Pennsylvania, Oregon, Nebraska, Wisconsin, Utah, Hawaii, South Dakota, Delaware, Virginia, Ohio, Arizona, Indiana, New Mexico, Connecticut and Michigan.
‡ West Virginia, South Carolina, North Carolina, Texas, Tennessee, Oklahoma, Pennsylvania, Louisiana and Arkansas.
§ New Mexico, Hawaii, Oregon, Florida, Minnesota, Idaho, Vermont, Delaware, Montana, Massachusetts, Maine, Michigan, Indiana. On these matters, see Bureau of Family Services, Dept. H.E.W., *Monthly Cost Standards Used By States for Specified Types of Old Age Assistance Cases and Families Receiving Aid etc.*

tations for a family of four on the basis of father, mother, and two children instead of for a mother and three children. Since an adult male costs more than a child to support, the minimum for a family of four would necessarily rise.

But these relatively inadequate state standards are only the beginning of the state reductions. For by state legislation and sometimes by administrative order the ceilings for what can be paid to the needy have been cut down still further. In the case of old-age assistance, this was done in no less than sixteen states. In ten of these the legally imposed ceilings were more than 20 percent below the state standards. In the case of aid to dependent children, the cuts made by the states were far more severe. There were nine states where the ceiling for aid was not reduced for the aged but was cut for dependent children.* In four states the ceilings for the aged were set at 20 percent or more below the state's own standard. In the fifteen states where the state standards were reduced for both categories, the greater severity of the cuts for children is shown by the comparison in Table 3.

While the severity of some of the cuts in the legal maximum for old-age assistance was marked, notably for those in Alabama, Alaska, Mississippi and Missouri, those for broken families with dependent children were far more severe and can even be termed as being predominantly savage. In nine of these states the legal ceiling for the children was less than half of the state's own standard, while in three more the percent reduction was between 25 and 35 percent.

There are certain states, however, that should be commended for not trying to cut their legal ceilings. There were no fewer than thirty-six that held steady legally on old-age assistance and twenty-two that maintained them for dependent children. New York, New Jersey, and Pennsylvania stood fast on both scores.

* These were California, Colorado, New Mexico, Ohio, Oregon, South Dakota, Texas, Vermont and Virginia.

TABLE 3

THE DEGREE TO WHICH LEGAL ALLOTMENTS
ARE REDUCED BELOW STATE-APPROVED STANDARDS *

State	*(1)* Old-age (single women)	*(2)* Dependent children (family of four)	*(3)* Percentage points by which maximum for children fell below that for aged (3) = (1) − (2)
Alabama	66	33	33
Alaska	50	43	7
Arkansas	79	46	33
Delaware	93	79	14
Florida	68	28	40
Georgia	91	62	13
Indiana	64	38	26
Iowa	92	75	17
Mississippi	50	21	29
Missouri	58	40	18
Nebraska	95	42	53
South Carolina	97	36	61
Tennessee	98	53	45
West Virginia	85	74	11
Wyoming	76	83	+7

But the real test is on the amounts actually paid in relation to need. This is frequently a third way in which the grants of assistance are reduced. The actual averages are not a perfect measure of this, since they omit from consideration the private incomes of the recipients and hence somewhat understate the total current resources. But they are a rough measure, as Table 4, on the next page, for September 1967 indicates.†

* For the sources of this material, see publications of the Social and Rehabilitation Service, Department of Health, Education, and Welfare, August 1967: *Old Age Assistance and Aid to Families With Dependent Children, Tables on Basic Needs,* etc.

† Compiled from Table M-24 in *Social Security Bulletin,* January 1968, p. 47.

TABLE 4

State and Region	(1) Average old-age assistance	(2) Average per recipient in families receiving aid to dependent children	(3) Average per person receiving general assistance
New England			
Maine	$ 53.65	$29.80	$13.85
New Hampshire	99.85	39.70	20.80
Vermont	71.20	42.80	——
Massachusetts	81.30	54.80	40.85
Rhode Island	61.00	44.25	28.75
Connecticut	76.30	47.45	28.45
Middle Atlantic			
New York	89.15	58.15	56.10
New Jersey	75.35	56.95	43.10
Pennsylvania	75.10	36.75	59.40
East North Central			
Ohio	66.25	36.95	33.95
Indiana	47.20	31.80	——
Illinois	60.80	42.85	40.15
Michigan	68.55	43.00	30.75
Wisconsin	63.05	48.65	28.20
West North Central			
Minnesota	63.90	52.60	28.20
Iowa	103.60	49.95	——
Missouri	68.45	24.90	50.95
North Dakota	77.80	46.25	13.15
South Dakota	62.45	42.00	10.65
Nebraska	57.75	36.90	——
Kansas	85.60	43.80	36.95
South Atlantic			
Delaware	64.45	32.00	29.00
Maryland	61.45	38.75	71.60
District of Columbia	73.20	38.20	80.35

(*Table continues on following page*)

175

TABLE 4 (Cont.)

State and Region	(1) Average old-age assistance	(2) Average per recipient in families receiving aid to dependent children	(3) Average per person receiving general assistance
South Atlantic (Cont.)			
Virginia	55.25	29.70	24.40
West Virginia	57.75	25.15	26.95
North Carolina	63.20	25.15	11.10
South Carolina	41.25	17.30	31.55
Georgia	51.40	25.45	14.20
Florida	49.70	15.35	—
East South Central			
Kentucky	56.55	28.15	—
Tennessee	52.80	26.80	11.95
Alabama	60.15	12.80	12.75
Mississippi	38.80	8.35	15.05
West South Central			
Arkansas	59.55	19.50	3.65
Louisiana	73.30	23.95	46.45
Oklahoma	74.35	34.45	—
Texas	58.90	21.50	—
Mountain			
Montana	65.00	38.30	19.55
Idaho	66.90	46.95	—
Wyoming	65.35	38.05	21.75
Colorado	80.25	37.85	12.35
New Mexico	57.35	30.70	26.30
Arizona	56.70	28.80	15.35
Utah	58.70	37.10	70.70
Nevada	72.05	30.70	23.45
Pacific			
Washington	68.85	46.70	48.70
Oregon	60.95	42.75	—
California	101.70	44.55	41.70
Alaska	72.05	34.90	16.10
Hawaii	78.00	44.00	54.65
Total United States	$ 68.60	$38.50	$38.85

In judging the relative adequacy of these sums, it should not be forgotten that approximately half of the 2.1 million who received old-age assistance were also receiving benefits from social security and that the minimum monthly grant under the insurance system was then $44.00. This, in itself, would therefore raise the average receipts from the government to $90 a month, or $1,080 a year. This average sum would be further increased by security payments in excess of $44 a month and by any other income of the recipients, whether in cash or in kind. In many places where aged people own their own homes, this fact is not fully taken into account in determining their monthly assistance grant, while they are also allowed to earn a supplementary income without full deduction.

Thus while many of the aged were being forced to subsist on inadequate sums and were below Miss Orshansky's poverty limits, they fared much better than the dependent members of families who were without a male head because of divorce or desertion.* The nationwide average payment for the members of this latter group was only $38.50 a month, or 56 percent of the average assistance grant for the aged. When it is remembered that the aged have supplementary income much more frequently than the dependent families, the disparity between the two forms of welfare payments is further accentuated. This is particularly marked in the South Atlantic and Southern states, for here not only are the proportions in the category of "dependent children" who are given relief below the nationwide average in many states but the actual sums allotted are also often grossly inadequate. Thus the average monthly allowance in South Carolina was only $17.30, in Florida $15.35, in Alabama $12.80 and in Mississippi the almost incredibly low figure of $8.35. These were averages of 58, 51

* There were also insurance benefits for widows and surviving children of males covered by social security.

and 28 cents per day respectively, whereas Miss Orshansky's standard called for $2.25 as the poverty floor for nonfarm and $1.58 for rural dwellers. Indeed, in thirteen states south of the District of Columbia, the average was less than $30 a month, or a dollar a day.

I again wish to emphasize the relative degree of social concern shown by such states as New York, New Jersey and Massachusetts, where the averages paid to members of dependent families were $55 a month or slightly more. These averages were nearly 50 percent ahead of the average for the country as a whole. In addition, the proportion of the child population aided in New York was also much above the national average.

There is, I believe, a connection between the fact that many of the states that pay more adequate sums for children have also been able to keep the proportion of the aged who receive assistance below the national average. Thus New York, New Jersey, Massachusetts and Connecticut probably stand at the top of the list so far as children are concerned, but these states also have an appreciably smaller proportion of the aged on assistance than is true of the country as a whole. This is shown by the fact that in the three states which cluster around New York City—New York, Connecticut and New Jersey—the percentages of those on old-age assistance were only from one-third to one-fifth that for the nation as a whole. The average grant for members of families with dependent children, however, ranged from 25 to 50 percent above the national average.

On the other hand, the states that had especially low grants for children tended to be relatively generous to the aged, whether in proportions or in amounts, or both. The Southern states along the lower Atlantic Coast as well as those in the South Central region paid low averages for a relatively small proportion of the children, but, as we have pointed out, they had a much larger proportion of the aged on the assistance rolls than the countrywide average. In the case of Georgia, Mississippi, Alabama, Arkansas, Louisiana and Oklahoma, this excess was from nearly three to over four times the national average. It is therefore suggested that in these latter states the children of broken families were slighted in order to cover more of the aged. This fact seems to be associated with the presence of a high ratio of Negroes in the population.*

The evidence from so many different comparisons is clear that the states have tended to be far more generous, or at least less niggardly, towards the aged than towards children in fatherless families. There are several reasons for this. The community tends to regard with some opprobrium families broken by divorce or desertion and to transfer to the mother and children some of the blame which should be attached to the deserting male. They also believe that many of the women in these broken relationships tend to be guilty of immoral conduct, and to be having additional illegitimate children at public expense. This is particularly true of the dominant attitude of the whites towards the Negroes. All this operates to reduce the amounts that are allowed by legislators and administrators and, in some cases, the proportions who are ruled eligible as well.

A very human second factor also operates in favor of the aged. Legislators and administrators can easily put themselves in the place of the needy aged. It is not hard for them to visualize that when they grow old they might lose their money and their children. They have seen many go through this unhappy experience.

This fellow feeling is largely lacking for the mothers and

---

* Thus in 1960 when the percentage of the total population in the country which was Negro was approximately 11.0, it was 22.5 percent in the South Atlantic states, 22.4 percent in the East South Central region, and 16.3 percent in the West South Central area.

children of broken families. Those who make the decisions for society have of course almost never gone through any such experience and they are suspicious of those who have. They therefore tend to slight them in the allotment of funds.

Finally, it must be confessed that, in all probability, political considerations operate to create the same biased treatment. Old people vote. Children do not. The aged are becoming better and better organized and a potent political force. The legislator or administrator who neglects them or discriminates against them does so increasingly at his peril. The old maxim that the squeaking wheel gets the grease applies here.

The children, however, do not know what is happening to them or who is doing it. Their mothers are hard pressed, poor, isolated, looked down upon, and often ignorant. It is almost impossible for them to combine, as can the aged, in self-defense or retaliation. They must suffer largely in silence or with only muttered complaints. Since they are largely indifferent to politics, which seems to have little or no connection with their lives, they tend to be neglected by the political structure, although the local party organizations and settlement workers at times take up their cause.

All this is not to say that too many of the aged get too much. The contrary tends to be true. But it is correct to say that the hapless children tend to be more neglected and to be relatively forgotten. They badly need to be helped, and they need this assistance to be more generous and more wise in its nature.

A second relatively neglected group are those in the active years of life who need help but who are at present debarred from receiving it. Those of us who helped to frame the original Social Security Act felt we were taking on enough when we provided for the unemployed and the aged and made at least a beginning at putting some support under the blind and the dependent families. Other types of poverty, we felt, had to be left either to individuals or to the states. The national government, we felt, could not be loaded down initially and simultaneously with all of these burdens. Gradually, as the way opened, needs became apparent, and as public opinion crystallized, additional categories of insurance and assistance were brought into the system, such as widows and orphans, the severely disabled, the self-employed in their old age, and finally—after a terrific and long drawn out struggle—we obtained hospital and medical care for the aged and for the medically indigent.

But those who, despite their efforts, were chronically unemployed, as well as those moving from farms and cities and across state lines, tended to be left out. So were those who worked for an inadequate yearly income or were burdened with large families. The federal government did little to help these millions of people, although it tried to help with the Wages and Hours Act and by its successive liberalizations, while if the states were to do so they had to do it alone.

The result, as we have emphasized, was relative neglect, both in numbers and amounts. All honor should be paid to such states as California, New York, New Jersey and Pennsylvania, which have tried to help these unfortunates. In fact, New York stands at the head of all the states in the care given to dependent children and those on general relief. But in the main, these categories were neglected and constitute the largest single gap in the social lines of protection against poverty.

If we take the some 9.1 million who are given various forms of relief and the several millions of the needy covered by social insurance, we probably have approximately 13 million. This is a little over 40 percent of the 30 million poor. If we were to include the unrecorded poor, it might be almost precisely 40 percent. The aid given to this group has not been sufficient to lift them out of poverty, although there are

probably several million others who have been so raised. It
does mean, however, that at least 60 percent or three-fifths
of the poor have not been reached at all by the systems of
social assistance and insurance, and that if we are to help
them, we need greater will, devotion and social intelligence.*

And perhaps I should make it clear that it is not solely the
fault of incomplete legislation that so many of the poor are
not covered. Many of the poor are ignorant of their legal
rights, or are ashamed or indifferent about testing them.
Others believe that the red tape of processing their applications is so time-consuming and humiliating that they either
do not apply or quit before the investigatory process is completed. Still others feel repelled by the coldness and imper-
sonality of those who deal with them.

It is worth while to inquire more minutely into the reasons
for this failure to cover more of the poor. The first main group
are those who are excluded from federal relief because of the
failure of Congress to include them among the categories
eligible for federal aid.

The fact that federal aid is provided only for those who
fall within the five separate categories throws upon the states
and localities the entire burden of caring for the needy who
do not fit within these categories. With the honorable exception of a few, the states have in general been reluctant to assume the burden of these general and noncategorized types
of relief.

More specifically, the major groups of the needy who are
legally excluded are the following:

1. Those barred by the residence and other eligibility requirements of the various states, including those who would

---

* The distribution of surplus foods, school lunches, and the food-stamp
program came in 1966 to a total of approximately $2 billion. In ad-
dition, private charity in the form of service and so-called character-
building agencies raised a total of over $550 million.

otherwise be eligible for old-age assistance and aid to dependent children.

2. Those who, for one reason or another, are "outside" the labor force.

3. Many of the unemployed, who were either originally ineligible for benefits or have exhausted their claims.

4. The families who are still in need even though their chief breadwinner is steadily employed.

5. Those forced into poverty by severe and uncompensated illness.

By failing to include these groups Congress and the country demonstrated a desire to move with extreme caution. They were reluctant to assume any financial responsibility for the care of these people and were afraid that such general public aid would greatly reduce the will to work.

A large group who are disqualified from receiving the categorical benefits are those who have not lived in a state long enough to meet the residence requirements. Because of the strong sentiment for states' rights, the federal provisions give a great deal of latitude in this respect to the states. The law on old-age assistance merely requires that no state shall impose a more restrictive residence requirement for the aged than that of one year immediately preceding the date of application and for more than five years out of the preceding nine. Within these somewhat ample maximum limits, the states are free to act as they wish.

There are fifteen states that take full advantage of both features of the federal maximum. As one might expect these include such states as California, Florida, Texas, Arizona, Washington, Colorado, Nevada, New Hampshire and Montana, which are particularly attractive to the aged who wish to retire.* The legislatures of these states have, therefore,

---

* The others are Arkansas, the District of Columbia, Oklahoma, Iowa, Kansas and Missouri.

wished to protect themselves against a possible flood of aged migrants whose active and tax paying years have been spent in other states.

The legislatures of these states have been afraid that liberal residence requirements would further stimulate this migration among the nonproductive age groups. This would burden their states because they would then be compelled to provide their share of the assistance grants. In spite of California's restrictions, however, there are 228,000 cases of old-age assistance in that state, who receive a comparatively generous average allowance of $102 a month. This is largely owing to the development of the aged as an active political force under the stimulus of Dr. Townsend and his successors.

There are three other states—Louisiana, Indiana and Ohio— that also require a year's prior residence, but they slightly soften the cumulative requirement to three instead of five years out of the preceding nine.*

The major group of states, twenty-six in number, impose only a one-year residence requirement without any cumulative feature. Among the most important of these states are Illinois, Maryland, Massachusetts, Michigan, New Jersey, Pennsylvania, Virginia and Wisconsin. †

The constitutionality of these provisions has been challenged by some states on the ground that they violate the principle of the equal protection of the laws. Some circuit courts have upheld that challenge and the issue is now before the U.S. Supreme Court.

* There were, however, 124,000 aged receiving assistance in Louisiana, receiving an average of $73. That state, since the days of Huey Long, has always been comparatively liberal in the treatment of its own aged.
† Several of these states provide modifications of these requirements if the states from which the migrants come make reciprocal concessions. The other states are Alaska, Alabama, Delaware, Georgia, Idaho, Minnesota, Mississippi, New Mexico, Nebraska, North Carolina, North Dakota, Oregon, South Carolina, South Dakota, Tennessee, Utah, West Virginia and Wyoming.

Finally, seven states waive all residence requirements and make the applicants immediately eligible. Four of these—Maine, Rhode Island, Vermont and Connecticut—are in New England, while the other three are Hawaii, Kentucky and, most meritorious of all, New York. New York, as we have seen, also provides a comparatively high average grant of $86 a month. In fact, as we have repeatedly pointed out, New York is the most humane of all the states and yet is not excessive in appealing to special interest groups.

The residence requirements for families with dependent children are slightly less severe than those for the aged, although still restrictive. The federal provision for this group is that no state can require more than a year's residence either by the child or the parent. There are forty-one states that substantially impose the federal maximum, though these are modified in a number of instances in favor of migrants who come from states with lower requirements.

There are ten states that waive all residence requirements. New York once again heads the list with 170,000 cases and nearly 700,000 recipients, of whom 510,000 are children. The others are New Jersey, Connecticut, Rhode Island, Vermont and Maine in the Northeast, and Alaska, Hawaii, Georgia and Kentucky.

The residence requirements of other states bar large numbers from welfare. There are comparatively few states that follow New York in its bold and praiseworthy assumption of national responsibility, although those in the Northeastern section of the country have shown the most commendable tendencies in this direction.

The record to date clearly shows the need for nationwide eligibility standards and for a lessening of the jealously guarded state separateness, but such a development will require the federal government to assume a much larger share of the total cost. It is greatly to be hoped that this will not require a centralized system of administration. For it is still crucially important for us to retain local interest and initiative, provided that this does not bring with it either discrimination or carelessness with public funds. The values involved are mixed, but it is, on the whole, the poor who suffer most from the restrictions. A national minimum graduated according to regional differences in the cost of living would certainly seem to be desirable.

For many years the families of the unemployed who had exhausted their claim to unemployment compensation were, as we have pointed out, completely ineligible for federally aided welfare payments. If these families were to be granted relief, the states and localities had to bear the full load. The result was that very few states would assume this financial burden. Therefore a man who still couldn't find a job when his unemployment compensation benefits stopped was not only out of luck himself but also brought continued misfortune to his family. Even though his wife and children might be in great need, they were disqualified from receiving welfare payments because they had a husband and father. If he deserted his family, however, they then became eligible for welfare payments under the category of aid to dependent children. Devoted heads of families were sometimes forced to "desert" in order to enable their dependents to be cared for. But if they were caught visiting their families, all was lost. There was said then to be "a man in the house" and the family was disqualified. It is impossible to conceive a worse set of provisions. Families were being broken up as a condition for relief and social workers were compelled to assume the role of detectives.

Our progressive group of Representatives and Senators made war on this provision during the 1950's, but we were always defeated. The majority continued to believe that the failure of a man to get a job after his initial period of unemployment compensation expired was his own fault. Neither he nor his family should be cared for, it was argued, lest his will to work be lessened and the doors to the federal treasury be opened.

Wives and children were, in effect, being held as hostages to stimulate a continued search for work on the part of husbands and fathers. But in 1962 we were successful in getting this group added to the list of those eligible for federal aid, so far as those who had exhausted their claim to benefits were concerned. Twenty-two states have accepted this provision, but twenty-eight have not. It is indeed strange that popular pressure has not forced more states to act, but in the majority of the states the old conditions still prevail.

The same fate befell the families of those who were ineligible on other grounds. Thus, as we have pointed out, hundreds of thousands have come to the cities from the farms where they have been tenants, farm laborers or small cultivators. When these migrants do not find jobs in the cities they have no record of covered employment behind them and they therefore cannot receive any unemployment benefits. Not falling within the specified categories, they and their dependents are also shut off from public relief or welfare payments, except in those cases where general relief is granted. Desertion is again the only other way by which such a man can provide for his family.

The most pitiable and indeed the most hopeless of all are those who have been unemployed for so long that they have given up hope and are no longer really hunting for work. They too are ineligible for relief. At the same time they are also used as horrid examples by the unsympathetic who seek to discredit the whole idea of granting federal or state aid to other groups of the needy.

The opinion-makers of the country have also been reluctant to admit that there are millions of Americans who work both hard and steadily but who do not receive enough to support their families. Yet we have seen in Chapter 5 that this is the case, and that there may be as many as nine or ten million in this group.

There has been a double opposition to the idea of supplementing the earnings of these men with welfare payments. It was argued that this would be in effect a subsidy for employers who paid low wages. This was hardly a valid objection in the case of self-employed farmers or possibly of farm tenants.

Second, few wanted to admit the fact that such widespread poverty existed among those who worked steadily. Finally, it would be extremely expensive for the state governments to assume responsibility for this group and to try to make good their personal and family deficits.

Instead the government, beginning in 1938, passed minimum wage requirements which, beginning with 25 cents an hour, rose during World War II to 40 cents. This applied to workers in manufacturing and the wholesale trade. Then in successive steps the minimum was raised for many occupations to 75 cents and then to $1.00, $1.20, $1.40 and finally $1.60. The original coverage was not appreciably extended until 1963 when it was broadened to include the larger retail stores and chains and finally, in 1966, to include hotels and restaurants.

But agriculture, where the earnings are particularly low, was excluded until 1966, when workers on the larger farms were brought under the act with an initial wage of $1.00 an hour. This was to rise gradually by 10 cents a year until it reached the general minimum of $1.60.

The general minimum of $1.60 an hour is the equivalent of $3,200 for a full time salary year of 2,000 hours. It therefore approximately meets the basic cost of a poverty standard for a family of four in an urban environment and does so for the nearly 41 million workers who are covered by it. It may be somewhat above the requirement for small towns and smaller cities, where it is quite possible that the Orshansky budget is something of an overstatement.

It has been charged that the increases in the legal minimum have made it more difficult for the less efficient workers to find employment. This does not seem to have been generally true prior to the 1965–66 increases, but it may have become partially true in the past two years. The area in which the greatest danger exists is in juvenile employment. Employers can pay those under eighteen years 15 percent less than the standard minimum for a period of six months. This may not be a sufficient inducement for the employers to hire unskilled and untrained workers who have not developed the work habits needed for modern industry. In practice, few such learners are taken on. The difficulties of the hard-core unemployed may, therefore, have been increased and this may be especially true among the young. A thorough review of this subject is badly needed, and some further allowance for young learners may be advisable. A half-century ago the exploitation of the young workers was a dominant problem. They worked long hours for low pay. The failure of so many of the young to get and hold a job is, however, the outstanding deficiency today. We should not allow old shibboleths to prevent us from facing this problem and dealing with it. It is better for this and other groups of the handicapped to be employed at a lower wage than to be unemployed at a higher theoretical wage, provided they do not bring down the minimum for competent adults. One immediate step is to train the presently unemployed and unemployable, and this the government is trying to do and should continue on an even larger scale.

A final group of the needy are the sick and their families who are not adequately compensated by private and public benefit plans and by medicaid. A praiseworthy beginning has been made in this direction in the last twenty years by large private companies and by the four states of New York, California, New Jersey and Rhode Island, but, as we have seen, much remains to be done and the number thrown into poverty from these causes is still high.

There are also reasons other than these legal disqualifications which prevent many of those legally eligible for assistance from obtaining it. Large numbers of the poor are ignorant and do not know where to apply for relief or are frustrated by the drawn-out process of applying and being investigated. Some, out of pride, refuse to apply and are resigned to go without aid. Others, as we have said, are repelled by the coldness with which they are treated. In other cases, the relief authorities themselves, in order to limit public expenditures, arbitrarily deny relief to many who both need and are legally qualified to receive it.

Whatever the reasons, it is still probably true that at least half of those in poverty, who badly need assistance, do not receive it. Indeed the proportion is probably in excess of one-half.

The so-called war on poverty proposed by President Kennedy and carried out by President Johnson has certainly diminished the number of the poor. Around $2 billion a year of federal money, in addition to relief and assistance, is now being spent on these programs, which are concentrated on youth. Headstart is being carried out for hundreds of thousands of preschool children; the Neighborhood Youth Corps for boys and girls in their teens provides useful employment on useful projects while enabling them to live at home; and finally the Job Corps, modeled in part on the CCC of the Depression years, gives work and training in separate camps for young men and women.

The Community Action Program also gives useful employment to hundreds of thousands of the older adolescents and adults, and widespread training programs have been carried out by the Department of Labor under the Manpower and Training Act. From 1962 up until June 1967, no fewer than 720,000 had been entered in this type of program, of whom 170,000 had been trained on the job and 550,000 given institutional training. The experience has been generally good, interspersed of course with many individual failures. Three-quarters of those institutionally trained were still retained a year after they first got a job, while nearly nine-tenths of those trained on the job were still hired and on the payroll.

However, the Negro poor in particular feel they have been left out. Historically, from the days of slavery on, they have been grossly abused by the whites, and it is only natural that they should resent this fact. They are looked down upon psychologically and in a sense ostracized not only because they are poor but also because they are Negroes.* They inevitably tend either to blame others or circumstances rather than themselves for their failure to advance and for their relative loss of ground.

The poor whites have something of the same feeling, but they do not suffer from the same psychological hostility on the part of others as do the Negro poor. They therefore are not as estranged from society and hence not as devoid of hope. But looming in the foreground now are the hundreds of thousands of youngsters from thirteen to sixteen who have

---

* Interestingly enough, the proportion of nonwhite poor who receive welfare seems to be greater than among the whites who were poor, namely, 33 percent as compared with 25 percent. A large part of this was undoubtedly due to the greater proportion of families headed by women among the nonwhites (23.7%) than among the whites (8.9%). But the statistics also indicate that at least in the North and West there is no proof that the Negro poor are discriminated against by the welfare authorities. See *Social and Economic Conditions of the Negro in the United States,* U.S. Bureau of Census and Bureau of Labor Statistics, 1967, p. 25.

almost given up trying to get ahead in school and who roam the streets, especially in summertime, without aim or employment. More and more they are being drawn into antisocial groups and acts by their elders.

It is true that there has been an impressive degree of progress. But this is scant consolation to the sixth or quarter of the population who have remained either in poverty or on its fringes. For while others have gone forward, those below the poverty level have not progressed. These members of the poor are little if any farther ahead than were their parents or grandparents. Indeed, surveys of the Watts area in South Los Angeles and of Hough in Cleveland seem to indicate that in these very poor black neighborhoods the relative amount of poverty has increased, as has the proportion of broken homes, while the percentage of unemployment has either decreased very little or not at all.*

The relative difference between the submerged sixth or the lowest quarter at the one extreme and the upper half on the other has therefore widened. Thus in 1947 only 6 percent of nonwhite families and 21 percent of the whites had incomes over $7,000 a year. By 1966 this had risen to 28 and 55 percent respectively. Outside the South the percentages were in fact 38 and 59 percent respectively.† The median income for families with a male head rose from $3,100 in 1947 to $7,235 in 1965. This was an increase of over 130 percent. But the average was drawing away from the bottom group.

Concerned citizens have come to feel a justified urgency about these many lacks in the welfare system and have tried to do something about it.‡

* *Social and Economic Conditions of Negroes in the United States,* U.S. Bureau of Census and Bureau of Labor Statistics, 1967, pp. x and xi.
† *Ibid.,* p. 17.
‡ Thus see the Report by the Advisory Council on Public Welfare, "Having the Power, We Have the Duty," 1966, 148 pp.

In 1967, the social security or insurance system was somewhat liberalized, while the public welfare system was tightened and made somewhat more stringent. The aged were given an across the board increase of 13 percent in security benefits at the same time that their monthly minimum was raised by 25 percent to $55. A 12 percent increase from $1,500 to $1,680 was provided in the amount a recipient could earn in a year without having his benefits reduced. Various other minor improvements were also granted. To finance these there was an increase in the contributions and in the benefit base from $6,600 to $7,800.

On the other hand, the welfare provisions for families with dependent children were restricted. (1) Mothers with dependent children were required to take work if child-care centers were provided for their children. Many of the liberals objected to the stringency of this rule, pointing out that if a mother had several children she should take care of them at home. More badly needed child-care centers may develop from this requirement, but the work provision needs to be wisely and humanely administered. (2) Far more questionable was the provision that federal aid would not be paid to any state for any larger proportion of children receiving aid than was the case during the first half of 1968. This completely neglected the fact that these numbers might increase because of interstate migration and a greater awareness by mothers of their legal rights. It is greatly to be hoped that these provisions may be modified or repealed and not merely postponed.

Taken together, the social security amendments of 1965 and 1967 increased the number of beneficiaries by approximately 2.1 million. The Social Security Administration believes that it will further reduce the number in poverty by about one and a quarter millions.

8 *Cash Supplements and Work for the Poor*

Many are so dissatisfied with the existing systems of social insurance and public welfare that they have sought alternatives in some form of guaranteed income or cash supplements for the poor, or in the concept that when all else fails the state should furnish work to the unemployed poor. Therefore, there are no fewer than four different sets of proposals advocated by those within this general group: an outright guaranteed minimum income, a negative income tax, children's allowances, and the state to be the employer of last resort. In their basic philosophy, all of these proposals have something in common with Ernest Hemingway's reply to Scott Fitzgerald, who, dazzled by his association with the rich, argued that the wealthy were innately very different from the mass of mankind. "Yes," Hemingway answered, "they have more money."

The main trouble with the poor, according to this group, is their poverty. Under the pressures of modern and especially city poverty, character degenerates and the will to work is weakened. Providing more income, it is argued, will meet the physical needs of life so that in the words of Browning, "Body gets its sup and holds its noise and leaves soul free a little." The advocates of these plans also generally wish to replace the current welfare system with them. Instead of having case workers investigate the actual "needs" of each family or individual, they would make the payments automatic once the needy have made a sworn affidavit of their income and the number of their dependents. Moreover, once granted, the state is not supposed to dictate how the money is to be spent. The poor are to make their own decisions and suffer for their own mistakes.

This cutting of red tape would certainly reduce the expense, delays and humiliations of public welfare. Those now disqualified by state residence requirements and by other restrictions would become eligible. So would those who are now denied welfare grants because they do not fall within the federally aided categories. Similarly, those who are uninformed or too proud to beg would be protected. The poor would have their poverty relieved in a self-respecting way—as a right and not as a charity. This, it is argued, would also greatly reduce administrative costs and a large number of case workers would be released for other activities.

There are other and more pedestrian arguments. Since the poor will have more money, they can buy more goods. This would supposedly enlarge the market for goods that would otherwise not be bought or produced, and this in turn would increase the demand for labor. By helping man as a consumer, the demand for him as a producer would be strengthened.*

This latter argument is sometimes based on a superficial assumption that there can be such a thing as general overproduction under our present system even if the price level is flexible. If prices, however, fall far enough as costs are reduced, the increased output could be absorbed. It is nevertheless true that if industry, because of agreements between producers, refuses to reduce prices when general costs are lowered through further mechanization, then more can be produced than can be bought at a given price level. Then if prices have not been subsequently reduced to attract more purchasers, the injection of increased monetary purchasing will indeed enable more goods to be demanded and hence produced at the same price level as before. In technical terms, the money-demand schedule will be shifted to the right so that at each and every price a greater quantity of the mass production goods will be demanded. In the real world of cartels and monopolies and of controlled prices and wage rates, an increase in the money demands of consumers may at times be needed to ensure full employment.

The general philosophy of the guaranteed income plan is fairly simple. So are the details. Once a guaranteed minimum is set for a family unit—let us say the 1966 poverty level of $3,365 for a nonfarm family of four, with variations according to the size of the family and regional and urban differences in costs, as well as changes in the cost of living—then the family is to be paid the difference between this sum and its actual income. Thus, if a family of four had an actual income of $2,000, the amount of the guaranteed yearly subsidy would be $1,365. If the family income was $2,500, then the yearly subsidy would be $865.

* This, for example, seems to be one of the chief arguments of Robert Theobald in his *Free Men and Free Markets*.

Miss Orshansky has made some estimates of the amounts needed to carry out this program. On the basis of the census sample for 1963, the total income required to maintain the 35 million poor on the minimum standard at that time of $3,160 would in that year have been $28.5 billion. The income of these same poor people in 1963 was estimated at $17 billion including welfare payments, so that the total amount of the subsidy needed then would have been $11.5 billion dollars. For 1966, the numbers of the poor were down to 30 or perhaps 32 million. This was about 5 million less than in 1963, a decrease of over a million and a half a year. At the same time, however, there had been an increase of about 7 percent in the cost of living. The total cost on a bare minimum would be around $27 billion. It is probably safe to say, therefore, that the total amount by which private income falls short of minimum needs for the entire population is now somewhere around $8 to $9 billion.

As I have already pointed out, since then the total amount of the welfare grants has also gone up somewhat, so that for 1966 they amounted to $4.3 billion * a year. In November 1967 the rate was $5.0 billion a year. The transfer of these welfare amounts to the guaranteed income account would make the specific cost of guaranteed income somewhere between $13 to $14 billion. If confined to families with children, the total cost would be at least $11 billion and possibly more.

The replacement of the welfare payments of $5.0 billions by the income guarantee would, of course, be a transfer and not an added cost on governmental budgets. Since, however, the state and local governments have been meeting about 40 percent of the welfare costs, it would relieve their budgets by around $2 billion a year and, hence, shift these costs to the

---

* *Social Security Bulletin*, May 1967, p. 35. This does not include vendor payments for medical service. These amounted to $2 billion in the same year (*ibid.*, p. 137).

federal budget. This would help the hard-pressed states and localities. In effect, the federal government would assume the cost of all cash grants to the needy instead of having a large share borne locally. This is, therefore, a further helpful by-product of the plan, although it should be recognized that complete federal support would undoubtedly carry with it either almost complete federal administration or, at the least, federally controlled administration.

An Appraisal of the Prospects for a Minimum Guaranteed Income

The proposal for a guaranteed income makes a genuine appeal to the conscience of the American people. It would seem to resolve the cruel paradox of widespread poverty in the midst of comparative plenty. But it is important to appraise its weaknesses before we make a final judgment.

First, a considerable amount of investigation will still be necessary. Not all of the sworn statements of income can be accepted at face value by the Internal Revenue Service. Any concealment of income by the recipients will be resented by their equally needy neighbors as well as by the comfortable classes, and so there will be a powerful demand to check the declarations of income. Without such a checking, federal spending could run wild. Any improvement over the existing system of inquiry will, therefore, be relative rather than absolute.

While there will be less checking of how the individual families spend their money, there will necessarily be some. It would be intolerable to let heads of families divert their allowances to liquor, drugs or other nonessentials instead of for food, clothing and shelter for their children. In practice, therefore, the government, despite the wishes of the present sponsors, would have to engage in some oversight of expenditures for the bottom-most sections of the nation. For the public would not permit the amounts they have contributed to be grossly abused by the recipients. And if the 9 million now receiving aid would be supervised less closely than they are now, the other 21 million in poverty would be inspected more closely. In other words, the 70 percent of the poor who now do not receive help under welfare plans would be subjected to more supervision than now. It is by no means clear, therefore, that the total amount of personal oversight by the state would decrease. It is even possible that the total might increase.

The chief criticism of the plan is that it would reduce the incentive to work. If for each extra dollar earned a dollar would also be subtracted from the family allowance, it would remove any economic reason for the poor to struggle upward to the poverty threshold. For every extra dollar gained, there would also be a dollar lost. And every dollar they lost in earnings would be made good by an added subsidy dollar. In this simple form, the plan would have the same built-in weakness which blights much of public housing and some of the relief programs; namely, it would encourage dependence upon society and discourage personal effort. It would also fully protect those who slackened in their zeal, so that they would rely upon the state to protect them from their own weaknesses and loss of income.

It was on this very account that several witnesses before Senator Joseph Clark's subcommittee, although they were statistically classed among the "poor," rejected any idea of the guaranteed wage. It seemed wrong, and indeed absurd, to them that a man who wouldn't work should be maintained by society. If this is the attitude of many of the poor, how much more so will it be the judgment of those in the various layers of the middle and upper economic classes?

Moreover, those who reach the upper limits of the poverty

level would still not be able to pay for decent housing. Some hidden subsidies in this field would still be necessary although this could be reduced if construction and operating costs could be drastically lowered.

Supporters of the plan brush aside these objections. They contend that there would be only a few such malingerers, and that, given the chance, most men and women would prefer to work and be self-supporting. They believe that the desire for the esteem of one's fellows would prevent this from being a fatal weakness. They also argue that once a family is brought up to at least the poverty level, life will not seem as hopeless as it does now and that ambition will grow. The poor will strive for more and in order to get more will work harder.

But to do this, it would be necessary to develop a more sophisticated formula than merely guaranteeing a basic income and then cutting the subsidy dollar for dollar when the earnings and private incomes of the poor rose. We would need instead to taper off the subsidies as income increased so that there would still be an incentive above the poverty minimum. To do this would mean that subsidies, even though lessened, would stretch into the ranks of the "near poor" and that total costs would correspondingly increase.

At present, most Americans are skeptical of the plan. They are afraid that a large proportion of the poor are just as lazy as they dare to be and that both the white and the black poor would take advantage of the plan. Besides, ingrained habits cannot be overcome merely by putting more money in a man's pockets. Those who are now poor despite their work and efforts might get a greater toehold on life. But there are many others who have been so demoralized by poverty that they would be largely content to remain where they are. Just as there were Private Schweiks in the Austrian Army who, despite military discipline, were skilled malingerers, there would be many more in a more relaxed civil society. And the presence and conduct of these malingerers might create so much hostility among the self-supporting sections of the population that they would propose and carry through a system of labor camps for those who did not try to work and ultimately to support themselves. Here, again, if such camps were properly conducted with a proper mixture of work, opportunity and humaneness, they could be very helpful. But what happened in labor camps run by the Nazis and Communists should make us aware of the dangers. Those camps were also originally touted as instruments for "reform and rehabilitation," but they ended up as places of torture and mass murder. No labor camp we might set up could be as terrible as that. But they might still be very brutal if we adopted in earnest the rule that Captain John Smith put into effect at Jamestown: "He who will not work, neither shall he eat." The public is not yet ready to accept the principle of the "Vagabond's Wage" once advocated by Bertrand Russell, which would go to those in need irrespective of whether or not they were actually trying to work.

But the major portion of the poor suffer from disabilities other than laziness. Forty percent of them are children, many of them physically or mentally handicapped. Others lack education and training. Poverty has itself handicapped nearly all of the young. Another five and a half million are men and women who are over sixty-five. Many of these cannot work full time. Others can only be fitted into jobs with great difficulty. Finally, many of the 10 million adults in the active years of life who are also poor suffer from disabilities and disease. Thus, there are nearly 700,000 who are either blind or adjudged "permanently and totally disabled"; and many more whose ills have not been discovered. Others have all kinds of personal disabilities, such as lack of education, language difficulties, racial prejudice, etc., to overcome. And we should not forget the millions who, though they work steadily at jobs, still cannot support their families.

More money is needed to help overcome these difficulties, but something more than money is also needed. Wise counseling would be a help, and a knowledge of how to utilize the supplementary services that are now available. In short, friendly assistance is still needed and the current unjustified disdain for social workers should not obscure their continuing importance.

The Negative Income Tax

To meet the problem of incentives, a number of economists, including Professor Milton Friedman, the former economic adviser to Senator Goldwater, have proposed what they term a "negative income tax," in which only a fraction of the difference between the poverty level and the income received would be paid by the government. Thus, if the private income of the standard-size family were $2,000, the amount of the governmental grant would be one-half of the 1966 income gap of $1,365, or $682, making the total income $2,682 instead of $3,365. This would cut the net cost in half to about $4 to $5 billion if the welfare payments were retained, or to a total of about $7½ billion if they were eliminated.

This cut in the income subsidy would have the advantage of giving the recipient an incentive to earn more money, since for every extra dollar which he earned, his outside benefits would only decrease by fifty cents, thus giving him a net gain of the remaining fifty cents.

Clearly, this proposal would not reduce the total number in poverty. It would instead, at best, merely cut in half the amount by which a recipient and his dependents fell below the poverty level. If, however, it were used as a substitute for the welfare grants, as some of its advocates desire, then many of the poor would actually receive less than they do now. For example, let us take a destitute mother with four dependent children who is today given an allowance of $2,000 a year towards the $3,365 she needs to attain even the poverty level. This is bad enough, since it meets only 60 percent of the poverty minimum. But since she has no private income to fall back upon, if the negative income tax were substituted for Aid to Dependent Children, she would then receive only $1,682 (i.e., half of $3,365) or $318 less than what she is now getting.

In some cases, therefore, the very needy would actually lose by such a plan. One way to correct this difficulty would be to have the proportion of the income gap to be met start at a relatively high percentage, which would then drop as the gap itself narrowed. Thus, it could be 75 percent for all incomes below two-thirds of the minimum, and then 50 percent of the gap between the two-thirds mark and the poverty level. Thus, a destitute family in such a situation would receive 75 percent of the first $2,200 ($1,650) plus 50 percent of the next $1,165 ($582), or a total of $2,232. This would still be less than an adequate amount; but, except in some cases in such generous states as New York, it would be more than the recipients are now receiving on public welfare. And there would always be an incentive for them to earn more. For up to the two-thirds mark, the recipient would retain 75 cents out of every dollar earned, and from there to the poverty level he would still retain 50 cents. Beyond the poverty level, in order to give some continuing incentive, the near poor could retain a third of each dollar earned up to near the upper limits of those in need though not in poverty. Roughly, these would be the near poor or those between $3,365 and $4,400.

· · ·

Children's Allowances

The third proposal is that of children's allowances.* This is now used in virtually all the countries of the Western world, including Great Britain, France, West Germany, Canada, Australia, New Zealand, etc. In all of these countries, it is a state system and is universal in its application and is not limited to a specific income class or to those who are employed by others. All parents are eligible.

This proposal also makes a deservedly strong appeal since it aims to protect the most severe and the most innocent casualties of poverty—the children—who form two-fifths of the total number of the poor. The costs of a system of universal children's allowances that would provide full maintenance for all children would, however, be staggering. If we take $500 as the minimum yearly cost of a child, then if this were given for all of the 70 million children who are under the age of eighteen,† the total bill would be approximately $35 billion a year. If the allowance was $550, the costs would

---

* It so happens that over forty years ago I proposed a modified form of family allowances for wage earners. See my *Wages and the Family,* 1925. Since industry at that time did not seem able to pay bachelors and heads of small families enough to support a family of five (which was then used as the standard), I proposed a basic wage that would be sufficient to support a man and his wife, and then paying an adequate allowance for all children up to a maximum number from an industrial pool, which would equalize the burden upon any one employer. This was to remove the danger of individual employers discriminating against those with children. My plan, however, did not adequately provide for the self-employed or for those who were outside the working force. And I may have erred in not sufficiently emphasizing the dangers of overpopulation, since I did not anticipate the great migration of the rural and nonwhite population into the cities.

† Of these, 20.4 million are under the age of five, 20.5 million are five to nine, and 19 million from ten to fourteen years inclusive. There are also approximately 17 million in the group from fifteen to nineteen years inclusive. I estimate that about three-fifths of these were in the ages from fifteen to seventeen inclusive, or 10.2 million. *Statistical Abstract 1966,* p. 8.

be just short of $39 billion. If the allowances were only paid for the 60 million children under the age of fifteen, the total annual cost on a $500 basis would be $30 billion, and on a $550 basis, $33 billion.

If the allowances were to be reduced still further to encourage some additional individual initiative and to help those among the near poor, the total costs would again be reduced. By fixing the allowances per child at $400 for the 8 percent of families in "abject poverty," $300 for the equal number in "poverty," and $200 for those on the "fringes of poverty," the total cost would be around $6.5 billion a year, if these sums were added to existing relief payments, and from around $7.5 to $8 billion if they served as a replacement.

With all the other demands that now press in upon the country, there would be little hope of raising any such sum. It would, moreover, be extremely wasteful to pay these allowances to the well-to-do. For in 1965, as we have pointed out, the upper fifth of the population with family incomes of over $10,000 received approximately 41 percent of the total personal income of the nation.* The topmost 10 percent with incomes over $13,700 received, indeed, 28 percent of the total. These families certainly do not need any additional subsidies from the federal government. Therefore, if family allowances are to be adopted, either their scale will have to be cut down for everybody or the number of recipients restricted. Some advocates of family allowances who believe in universal payments also advocate an added tax on the upper incomes which would take back most, if not all, of the allowances paid to them.

There would also be some borderline cases of injustice where the allowances plus the other income would exceed the incomes of those who were just above the line. To remedy this would take a minute series of adjustments, which would

* *Statistical Abstract 1967*, pp. 332–33.

not only be hard to effect from an administrative standpoint but might also involve a probing into private affairs which the newer systems are intended to avoid.

Daniel Moynihan, one of the foremost advocates of children's allowances, recognizes the difficulties. Preferring to make the allowances universal in order to remove the stigma of charity from the recipients, he proposes that, according to the Canadian model, they be reduced to $8 a month for children under the age of five and to $12 for those from five to seventeen. If universalized, this would cost $9 billion a year. This cost would be manageable in a period of peace. But it would also pay unneeded surplus to the well-to-do, while only meeting a fraction of the cost of children in the families of the poor.* It would meet the ironical social standard that before the poor can have a mouthful, the rich are to have a banquet.

The question arises, therefore, whether it would not be better to build upon an improved and humanized system of public assistance, employment and training, than to depend upon a system of more or less automatic cash supplements.

All three of the cash-income plans would help to divert attention away from the older systems of social security, public aid, training and employment, which have been so painfully built up during the last third of a century. This is the very explicit aim of the conservative advocates of the negative income tax. They would scrap not only public aid, but also public and subsidized housing, recreation, public health, and other aids to those of low income.†

By giving the poor inadequate sums, which in order to in-

---

* Someone has come up with the idea of a children's allowance in reverse, namely, to pay mothers under forty-five, particularly those who have already had three children, so much for each year in which they do not have children.

† But this, of course, is not the aim of the more liberally minded among the advocates of cash supplements.

crease their incentive to work would still keep them below the poverty level, the conservative wing of the movement would be largely able to wash its hands of any further moral responsibility. Many would even go so far as to argue that if these cash grants were given, then not only public aid but also social insurance and public education as well should be abandoned. People could then be cast adrift to rely solely on their own resources and initiative. The market, with all its inequalities, would reign supreme and be unhampered in the provision of goods and services.

This proposal ignores the obvious fact that human beings need not only an individual cash income but, as Michael Harrington has properly stressed, social income as well. Indeed, the poverty budgets themselves presuppose the existing systems of public education, health, recreation and other facilities, which are supposed to be as available to the poor and their children as they are to others. Take them away and the minimum would have to be raised.

Some of these services, such as recreation and much of public health, could not be replaced on a voluntary basis even if the community were to abandon them. Central Park for example could not be purchased by the voluntary contributions of the poor, nor would the poor chip in enough to provide for clinics and visiting nurses. In other cases such as education, even if the present poverty level were met, private incomes would not be enough to meet the tuition and other costs were these services to be put on a so-called self-supporting basis. For the yearly cost per pupil in the public and private elementary and high schools of the country in 1965 was approximately $540. A family living on the poverty level of $3,365 could not pay this sum for the education of each of their children. Moreover, even if all the families were brought up to the poverty level, the resultant $60 to $65 a month that they could spend for rent would not under present costs provide them with decent housing in our cities. If we were to give up the collective purchase of services such as the public schools, health care, and parks and playgrounds, we would then have to revise upward the estimates of how much private income is socially necessary, and to do so on a marked scale. This would greatly increase the cost of these proposed plans, although still failing to meet man's basic needs. Public opinion has long since accepted the idea that children should have the effective right and opportunity to go to school, to be inoculated against disease and have their health protected, to play in the parks and go swimming in pure waters.

For these and other reasons, the provision of any added cash grants to the poor should not be treated as a substitute, but rather as a supplement to the existing social income that is rightfully theirs. In fact, these forms of social income should be not merely maintained but increased.

So, indeed, should public assistance or welfare. It should be stripped of its present humiliating, ugly and unintelligent features. It can and should be improved, humanized and made more effective.

A distinguished and competent Advisory Council on Public Welfare made a report in 1966 that advocated such a thoroughgoing revamping. It recommended that the various separate welfare categories be abolished and that adequate assistance be granted to all who were in need in accordance with nationally—not state—determined standards. In other words, home or general assistance was to be recognized equally along with the present categories. The federal government was then to assume the financial responsibility for meeting these standards, and was to assess the states in accordance with a formula that the council said "should recognize the relative fiscal capacity of the federal and state governments to finance adequate and comprehensive programs" and would "provide for equitable and reasonable fiscal effort among states." * No estimate was made of the probable total costs of such a program, nor was any specific formula developed for sharing the costs. It was apparent, however, that the share of the various states would vary in some inverse ratio to their per capita personal income.† The federal government would meet the difference between the costs of providing the federal standard to the needy in each state and the amounts that the state would be expected to contribute under the formula.

In order to help promote the mobility of the population and make the needy eligible, it was recommended that the various state requirements for prior residence be abolished, along with other arbitrary requirements for eligibility. Recent decisions of the federal courts in Connecticut and the District of Columbia have declared that the imposition of residence requirements deprives individuals of the guarantee of the Fifth Amendment that no state is to deprive any person of his equal rights and privileges under the law. If these decisions are upheld by the Supreme Court, then the abolition of the residence requirements will be greatly speeded up.

If and as this is done, there will be an increasing demand that the federal government assume a greater degree of financial responsibility and support, and with this there will be a strong tendency toward making the scale of benefits more uniform from state to state.

The President's Advisory Council also recommended that while the present financial roles of the state and federal governments should be reversed, the states were to be retained as the main administrative units. But in return for the federal government's assuming the larger share of financing, they were

---

* Report, Advisory Council on Public Welfare, 1966, p. 33.
† This ratio could also be modified by a second ratio of the percentages of per capita income spent in each state for these purposes.

to pledge prompt and available action on applications, set up an independent appeals mechanism, and give welfare clients legal counsel if requested.

This thorough and humane report may influence future public opinion. It helped President Johnson to make his series of excellent recommendations to Congress during the winter of 1967, which not only urged more aid to children and the aged but also dealt with specific problems in the fields of education and poverty.

The program should not be brushed aside. It deserves our understanding and support as citizens. It has met with the opposition of the conservatives, who do not believe in federal efforts to diminish poverty. Sometimes this opposition is noisy and open, but more often it is quiet and effective, aiming either to cut off or reduce the funds that are necessary to carry out the program.

Along with this criticism from the right, the program has also been subjected to a drumfire of disparagement from the left. Part of this attack is reasoned and basically idealistic. But part reflects the quasi-anarchism that characterizes much of the thought and actions of the so-called New Left. There is nothing so frustrating to a politician who is honestly striving to help the public than to face this crossfire from mutually contradictory sources, which when united in opposition can prevent any forward movement at all. The impossible best is often the worst foe of the practicable better.

The public should therefore study the facts and causes of poverty, understand the various proposals and enlist actively in the support of that which is most practicable. If we were to do this, we could be sure of a much more favorable response from Congress, the various state legislatures and the hard-pressed governors and mayors than we are otherwise likely to get.

While I believe the President's general program is worthy

of our support, there are certain features, some explicitly stated by him and some that may be implied, that are especially important. For example, much of the humiliation that is now bound up with the investigations of income would be avoided if only a sworn statement of income by the applicant were substituted for the present detailed questioning by case workers. This has not only been suggested by Welfare Commissioner Ginsberg of New York City, but has been put into effect in two of the welfare districts of that city. It would do a good deal to decrease the hostility that the recipients of assistance have quite generally developed toward their case workers. A special unit of the Internal Revenue Service could be given the job of checking on violators and relieving the Welfare Department of this responsibility. This would help the case workers to seem more like informal friends of the recipients instead of detective-investigators. In the first month of trial in New York, only one fraudulent case was found among approximately four thousand. The close supervision over expenditures could also be lessened.

A second need is to increase the amount of the federal grants and the share of federal support. These should be so combined as to reduce the total burden now borne by those states and localities which are making an honest and humane effort to help their poor. I would suggest that within an increased total, the percentage of cost borne by the federal government should be increased from one-half * and should vary between two-thirds and nine-tenths. If a state paid out in welfare assistance a given minimum percentage of its per capita income, the percentage of the federal contribution of the total could be varied inversely with this income. The poorest eligible state would then have to pay only 10 percent of its total costs, while the wealthiest would pay 33⅓ percent. But

---

* It is about 60 percent in the case of the aged.

these percentages would be subject to the general rule that each state should have its total welfare burden reduced.

In return for all this, the states should then drop their residence requirements, provide an impartial appeals tribunal, and live up to at least their own paper standards of relief. Desirable as it is to abolish all welfare categories and to treat "need" as such according to national standards, this may not be practicable at the moment. For in the process, it would reduce the relative, and in some cases the absolute, favored positions now enjoyed by some of the aged and the blind, who are two of the strongest and most articulate of the beneficiaries. I personally would favor including all "general" assistance among the federally aided, but if this is politically impossible, I would like to include at least all the children of the genuinely unemployed, namely, those able to work, willing to work, and seeking morally and physically "suitable employment." * I would do this without regard to whether or not the parents were eligible for unemployment compensation. And I would also include the children of those who because of disability or sickness are unable to work steadily. This would leave for the future the knotty problem of what to do for the children of those heads of families who, although able to work, were not

* There are at present 22 states with a total population of about 118 million which grant assistance to families of breadwinners who have exhausted their claims to unemployment compensation benefits. In February of 1968, these assistance grants were being made to 78.5 thousand families with a total of 441,000 members, of whom 295,000 were children. The February payments amounted to $17 million, or $217 per family and $38.70 per recipient. These grants really helped the large families of unemployed workingmen. There are, however, 28 states with a total population of 82 million which do not provide this assistance. These include all thirteen Southern states, four Midwestern states—Indiana, Missouri, Iowa and Minnesota—eight states of the high plains and mountains, and two northern New England states—Vermont and New Hampshire. The great industrial state of New Jersey is without such a law, and the numbers on the rolls in Maine, Rhode Island, Kansas and Nebraska are merely nominal.

actually trying to do so. In general, I do not like to see children used as hostages for their parents.

Perhaps most important of all would be a co-ordinated program of providing work and training for those on public assistance who are able to work, and which would also reach the unemployed who for one reason or another are not part of the working force. Part of this involves giving financial incentives by allowing recipients to keep a given amount of outside earnings and then retain a diminishing fraction of additional increments. There should also be special efforts by the public employment officers to place those relief clients who are properly qualified. These people cannot expect, as they sometimes do, to start at the top or even in the middle or lower-middle layers of industry. They should be prepared to accept initially humble but useful jobs in preference to remaining completely idle for long periods of time, holding out for those rare openings that will probably never come and that a large proportion would be unable to fill properly if they did. But as they get a foothold on a working life, they can prepare themselves for better jobs and they should be given an opportunity to do so. Some of the working time should be set apart for basic education to the degree needed.

Thus there should be a rapid extension of the training given under the Manpower Training and Development Act. This should include many groups, such as (1) youngsters who have not been able to find a job and have been idle, (2) young people employed in private industry and the Neighborhood Youth Corps, (3) mothers who need more skills for housekeeping, cooking and the care of children, as well as more general education and a greater ability to do part-time service work and (4) older workers who have been displaced from their former jobs and need to be retrained. The last should include not only those temporarily frozen out from urban jobs, but also those who have been displaced from agriculture and are now forced to seek nonfarm jobs. We are making more progress in the first two of these fields than the general public realizes. But we can and should do still more, both for them and for the latter two groups.

Aid to the families of dependent children is probably the most unpopular of all public welfare programs. But if the mothers were given training in the care and feeding of their children and in simple cooking, nutrition and housekeeping, the program would be immeasurably improved. Under the inspiration of the late Ray Hilliard, Chicago has pioneered with great success in this field. But the work is worthy of wider application and the new Social Security Act will help in this direction. By dividing a group of mothers in a neighborhood into two or more subgroups, one of which would take care of the children while the others would receive a short training course and then alternate with the others, the standards of the whole group could be rather quickly raised. Those who proved to be the best in child care could then permanently take care of the children in the neighborhood during the day, thus releasing the other mothers to work for wages. Part of the net pay of the mothers could then be used for the care of their children while the remainder of their income would raise the standard of living of their families. They could retain two-thirds of any net increase. If this were managed efficiently, the children and mothers would be better off; the mothers would become more capable and hopeful, and the government would also save some money as private earnings replaced a portion of the federal-state grants.

Along with all this should go efforts to improve the morale among the social workers. This would involve reducing the average number of persons assisted by each worker and, at the same time, stressing the constructive ways in which social workers can help people in trouble. Community referral and aid centers are essential for making known to the poor all the resources of the neighborhood and city in such fields as health, recreation and education.

Along with all these improvements, the poor, like others, would be immeasurably helped by the development of a greater sense of neighborhood. It is almost impossible for most people to feel deeply loyal to and personally identified with our huge metropolitan areas of half a million or more people. Even a quarter of a million or perhaps a hundred thousand are too many. In these cities the individual tends to feel lonely, isolated and, indeed, alienated. This is especially true if people are housed in high-rise apartment buildings rather than in individual homes. In these huge cities, public opinion does not operate as a restraining force upon individual conduct, nor does one find many neighbors who are helpful in trouble. It would improve city life if we were to build up communities of from 30 to 75 thousand people within the big cities, each of which would have its own schools, playgrounds and parks, its fire and police forces, its sanitation and health units, its welfare activities, etc.—and where the public interest could be represented by community councils, churches, civic groups, employers, labor unions, and the political parties. In other words, a decentralization of many of the administrative functions of a city within a framework of general standards of performance would help to develop a greater sense of community. And in this work, the citizens of the neighborhoods should be active partners and participants. The development of four- and six-block neighborhoods effected through the transformation of some street and alley space into inward-looking green areas and pocket parks would be very helpful.

I believe the main thrust of our poverty program should be along these lines. We can then find out whether greater protection to the needy reduces the human incentive to effort and whether it causes an undue increase in the birth rate or any adverse tendency in human selection. Family planning should certainly accompany any increased aid to the larger families. Meanwhile, we should not suspend our desire to help those who suffer until the last fastidious objection has been overcome. If we were to so refrain, the will would be paralyzed and we could not move forward. There is a wisdom in human action, which was well stated by Pascal. "The heart has its reasons which reason knows not of." Let us act, but let us also be always conscious of where we are going and of the difficulties along the way.

During this period, we can further examine the proposals for automatic guarantees of income to the poor, especially in the field of children's allowances for the poor or allowances in reverse, and we can make limited experiments in those directions. A city, for example, could be authorized to start such an experiment under the Office of Economic Opportunity so that the effects upon the care of children, the efforts of parents and the birth rate can be carefully studied. Such experiments are one of the advantages of a true federal system, which permits the cities and states to experiment beyond an agreed minimum of national effort. Federal aid can help in this direction.

As we experiment with children's allowances, it might be well if we also tried to guard against the possible danger of overpopulation on the part of the more thoughtless sections of the community. This could be done by not paying allowances for children beyond the third or fourth and by extending the opportunities for birth control and family planning. Three children is about the number needed to provide for a stationary population after allowing for early deaths, bachelors and spinsters, together with childless marriages and those marriages which produce only one or two children. It is not at all clear that children's allowances would stimulate a higher birth rate, but to the degree to which they might, any such incentive would be lessened or removed by imposing a ceiling on the number of children per family for which the allowances would be paid.

A final proposal is that the federal government should become the employer of last resort by guaranteeing to furnish a job, either in public or private employment, to all those able and willing to work. It is not always stated what the wage should be, but it should be enough to provide a minimum for the worker. This would presumably be the basic federal minimum wage of $1.60 an hour, or $3,200 for a year of 2,000 hours. Allowances for a reasonable number of additional dependents could be added to this if desired. Youngsters without dependents could be paid less. All this would provide a guaranteed income to the people while obtaining in return useful services and needed public works.

The nearest approach to this in the past was the W.P.A. (Works Progress Administration) of the Depression years. This experiment has never received its just tribute from writers and commentators and its initials are commonly used as a term of disparagement. But for a total cost of approximately $10 billion, the W.P.A. erected 25,000 public buildings and in addition constructed:

> 651,000 miles of highways, streets and roads
> 78,000 bridges and viaducts
> 24,000 miles of sidewalks and paths
> 35,000 stadiums and grandstands (and improved 90,000 others)
> 7,000 parks and playgrounds (and improved 17,000 others),

while a multitude of other useful works was also done.

In addition, work of this nature built up the strength and abilities of those who would otherwise have been unemployed.

It is interesting and perhaps significant that the "Urban Coalition," consisting of nearly a thousand civic, labor, business and local government leaders, at their meeting in the summer of 1967 endorsed this proposal to make the government "the employer of last resort." Senator Joseph S. Clark followed this up with a proposal to spend approximately a billion dollars a year more to help carry out the principle, and while this amendment was defeated on the floor of the Senate, it polled a significant number of votes.

Since there is also a natural reluctance to having the government assume an unlimited liability in serving as the employer of last resort, this could be moderated by fixing a definite maximum number of the additional jobs to be created. If a million such jobs could be created, the major portion of the unemployed among the juveniles and displaced farm workers would be absorbed. If private industry would guarantee to absorb half of these, and train them in such service trades as hotel and restaurant service, chauffeurs and auto mechanics, dental aides, etc., the creation by the government of the other half million jobs should not be too difficult. Girls and young women could be productively employed as nurse's aides and public health assistants. Both men and women could be trained as teachers' assistants. The energies of young men could be channeled constructively by hiring them, as the National Crime Commission has recommended, as apprentices in police departments. There is also a need for constructive work in cleaning up vacant lots and cleaning streets and alleys. This work is in no sense demeaning. The Neighborhood Youth Corps and the Community Action Program of the Office of Economic Opportunity have been very helpful in this work, and if given adequate funds can be more so. Philadelphia has done especially well in building and equipping postage-stamp playgrounds and parks. Some are as small as 18 by 60 feet, equipped with a circular "jungle gym," a slide and another simple apparatus. Supervision is by a committee of residents in the block. Quite beautiful gardens of flowers and shrubs have also been created and maintained. In all these efforts, community interest, support and participation are essential. The creation of these 500,000 additional jobs would cost about $2 billion a year for wages and materials.

I personally believe that the nation should also guarantee the annual construction of 500,000 additional housing units over a ten-year period for the poor, near poor, and lower middle class. Private industry could assume responsibility for some of these, through an extension of the co-operative principle, and the federal, state and local governments the remainder. As one of the conditions for awarding these contracts, which would increase the incomes of both builders and craftsmen, it should be required that a given percentage of slum youths be engaged as laborers or learners. A reasonable estimate would be that each additional housing unit above the present rate could use from one-third to one-quarter a man-year of such additional labor. This would create from 125,000 to 160,000 added jobs in the construction industry, to which would be added the indirect stimulus given to employment in industries producing building materials and supplies.

Such proposals as these would greatly increase the sums now spent for welfare purposes. I estimate that this increase would amount to at least $8 to $10 billion a year more than is now expended. This may seem sharply opposed to the prevailing drift of public and political opinion and to be inconsistent with the present costs of the war in Vietnam. It is unfortunately true that many of the more affluent groups in the suburbs are developing a bitter dislike for the poor and especially for the Negro poor. Many of these critics believe that most of the poor are lazy, improvident, sexually unrestrained, and given to violence. The critics believe that these qualities are innate and that it is these faults of the individual which are primarily responsible for poverty. They therefore do not believe that these defects can be removed speedily or even ultimately by improvements in the social environment. They are consequently opposed even to spending as much money as we now do for welfare, education, training and housing. A big increase would be even more bitterly opposed by them.

The strength of this reaction was evidenced, I believe, in the 1966 elections and in the behavior of the Congress that was chosen at that time. Virtually every one of the forty-seven Democratic members of the House who were defeated in 1966 was a Democratic liberal from the North and West who supported the principles of the war on poverty. In nearly every instance, they were replaced by more conservative Republicans. The long-standing coalition between the conservative Southern Democrats and the conservative Republicans was correspondingly strengthened, and the results were clearly seen in the roll-call votes by which many features of the welfare measures were initially curtailed. The members of the conservative coalition certainly do not want those who have good jobs and comfortable incomes to be taxed more heavily than they are now in order to take better care of more low-income people.

On the whole, the bloody riots of 1967 and 1968 have served temporarily to polarize and intensify the feelings of both blacks and whites. They have deepened the bitterness of many Negroes, who form one-ninth of the total population. At the same time, they have also intensified class and racist feelings among many in the other eight-ninths of the population. Perhaps the assassinations of Dr. King and Senator Kennedy may moderate these feelings and lead to a greater degree of concern and reconciliation. But unless this happens, I must admit that the prospects for greater social concern in the next few years are not favorable. Acts and sentiments in the immediate future may become worse rather than better. And in the process, reforms such as those I have advocated may wither.

But I cannot believe that such a philosophy will permanently predominate in an America which for nearly two centuries has, on the whole, increasingly devoted itself to realizing the principle of equality of opportunity and the basic worth-whileness of human beings. This basic decency of the vast majority of the American people has enabled us in the past to overcome temporary epidemics of racism and class prejudice. We have absorbed successive waves of immigrants, often of widely differing cultures and ways of life and have drawn them into the bloodstream and mainstream of American life.

In spite of all the difficulties created by biological differences in color and by cultural inheritance, I am sufficiently optimistic to believe that we can overcome our present problems and come safely into harbor. Certainly the will to believe that this is so makes the goal more possible to attain. Therefore as individuals we should do what we can to help this come about. And if it is objected that the war in Vietnam now prevents our launching out on such a program, we should ask ourselves which is more important, to put a man on the moon and get him back or help to make life here on earth better? Should our attention be centered more upon Venus and Mars than upon Newark, East St. Louis and Detroit? Is it more pressing to spend billions of dollars so that the jet set can save time in getting to London and Tokyo than it is to make our cities more livable? Should the oil millionaires of the Southwest be given hundreds of millions and indeed billions of dollars in tax favors in preference to helping to train, educate and house the poor?

Finally, the war in Vietnam will someday come to an end. When it does, $30 billion a year will be released. Should not a portion of this be used to help wage war on poverty? And what about the enormous increases in land values created by the growth in population but legally appropriated by the owners of strategic pieces of land? Should they not be used, in part, to further the progress of the larger community which has created them?

And finally, we would do well to remember the words of Tolstoy: "The trouble comes because some people feel that you can deal with people without love, and you can't. One may deal with things without love, one may cut down trees and hammer iron without love. But you cannot deal with men without it. Just as you cannot deal with bees without being careful." The increasing crescendo of riots in our cities during these last three years is not only a corroboration of Tolstoy's thesis, but also in a sense a mandate that we practice a more fraternal way of life. The future of America largely depends on what our answer will be. The way will not be easy. But the task is important.

Index

Affluent Society, The, 124

Aiken, Sen. George, 72

allowances, children's, 194, 195, 204–208, 216

American Bankers Association, 97, 111, 112

American Bar Association, 97

Americans for Constitutional Action, 81

Americans for Democratic Action, 81

Anderson, Sen. Clinton P., 51

Anderson, Paul Y., 51

Anti-Monopoly Committee, Senate, 36

Anvil Points, Colorado, 31, 32, 33, 34, 44, 58, 60

Banking and Currency Committee, Senate, 96, 97, 100, 119

Barry, Frank, 48, 49, 66

Beame, Abraham, 75

Bennett, Sen. Wallace F., 98

Bergson, Henri, 90

Black, Hillel, 98

bonds, state and local government, 17–18, 92

Bowery Savings Bank of New York, 107

Bradley, Douglas, 44

Brooke, Sen. Edward, 100

Browning, Elizabeth Barrett, 195

Bureau of Land Management, 67

Buy Now, Pay Later, 98

campaign donations, 12, 76, 77, 78

campaign expenses, 71–85

candidate grants, 79–84

Carey, William L., 3

Carroll, Sen. John A., 55
Carver, Thomas Nixon, 22
Case, Sen. Clifford, 97
Cervi, Eugene, 44
Civilian Conservation Corps (CCC), 156, 190
Clark, Sen. Joseph, 199, 218
Cleveland Cliffs Corporation, 32
Coleman case, 66, 67, 68
Communications Act, 51
Community Action Program, 190, 218
conflict of interest, 91
Connally, Sen. Thomas, 2, 10
consumer credit, 95–121
Consumers' Advisory Board, 96
Continental Oil Company, 32
Conquest of Mexico, 25
Conquest of Peru, 25
Cooley, Frank G., 45
COPE, 81
Cordon, Sen. Guy, 52–53
credit price competition, 116, 117, 118
Credit Union National Association, 102
crushing method (oil extraction), 34–36

D. A. Shale case, 69
De Gaulle, Charles, 107
dependent children, aid to, 155, 161, 162, 163, 166–167, 168–182, 185, 186, 193, 203, 210, 212, 214

depletion allowance (on gas and oil), 9–14, 59, 62, 63, 143, 221
depreciation allowances (on buildings), 19–20
Dillon, Douglas, 6
disclosure of funds, public, 92, 93
Dodd, Sen. Thomas, 79, 89
Dodge, Mrs. Horace, Sr., 17
Douglas amendment (oil depletion), 11–14
Dulski, Rep. Thaddeus, 79
Duncan, Robert, 75

Economic Advisers, Council of, 124, 126
Economic Committee, Joint (congressional), 3, 5, 132
Economic Opportunity Act of 1965, 123, 143
Economic Opportunity, Office of, 124, 216, 218
Election Financing, President's Committee on, 84–85
Eliot, Charles W., 127
Elk Hills, 51
Emerson, Ralph Waldo, 92
Ethics Committee, Senate, 79, 92

Fall, Albert, 42
Federalist, The, 26
Finance Committee, Senate, 2, 3, 6, 8, 12, 24
Finney, E. C., 42

Fisher, Joseph, 55
Fitzgerald, F. Scott, 194, 195
Fleeson, Doris, 3
Fleming, Roscoe, 55
Foster, Dr. William T., 95
Freeman, J. R., 44, 45, 49
Friedman, Milton, 202

Galbraith, J. Kenneth, 55, 124
Garnsey, Morris, 55, 65
Garula case (*Udall v. Garula*), 66, 67
George, Sen. Walter, 2
gifts, 89, 90
Ginsberg, Welfare Commissioner Mitchell, 211
Goldwater, Sen. Barry, 202
Gore, Sen. Albert, 3, 4, 6, 8, 12, 14, 16, 26, 80, 81 84
Great Treasury Raid, The, 5, 23
Gross National Product (GNP), 12, 143, 146, 147
guaranteed minimum income, 194–201, 206, 207, 208, 216, 217

Halpern, Rep. Seymour, 120
Harding, Warren G., 51
Harrington, Michael, 123, 126, 128, 150, 207
Hart, Sen. Philip, 55
Hatfield, Gov. Mark, 75
Headstart, 190
Hemingway, Ernest, 194, 195
Hill, Sen. Lister, 52
Hilliard, Ray, 214

History of Interest Rates, The, 100
Homer, Sidney, 100
Humble Oil Company, 32
Humphrey, Sen. Hubert H., 1, 3, 10

Ickes, Harold L., 42, 52
in situ method (oil extraction), 36–38, 61, 64, 65
interest rate, annual, 113–118
Interior Committee, Senate, 45, 48, 49, 66
investments, 91, 92
Ivanhoe, 27

Job Corps, 190
John Birch Society, 81
Johnson, Lyndon B., 123, 190, 210

Kelley, Ralph S., 41
Kennedy, John F., 6, 123, 190
Kennedy, Sen. Robert F., 85, 220
Keyserling, Leon, 126, 128
King, Dr. Martin Luther, 220
Kroll, Cedric, 108, 110

La Follette, Sen. Robert, Jr., 26
La Follette, Sen. Robert M., Sr., 26, 51
Lampman, Robert, 128
Laughter, 90
Leacock, Stephen, 100, 110
leasing rights, oil and mineral, 58, 59, 60, 66–69
Lehman, Sen. Herbert, 26, 78

Levin, Murray, 75
Lindsay, Mayor John, 75
Long, Sen. Huey P., 169
Long, Sen. Russell, 80
Lubig, Donald, 6
Lynch, Daniel, 44, 55

MacDonald, Dwight, 123, 126, 128
McEwan, Father, 99
Madison, James, 26
Magee, Carl, 51
Manpower, Training and Development Act, 191, 213
Manvel, Allen, 22
medicaid and medicare, 157, 158, 159, 160, 181, 183, 189–190
Metcalf, Sen. Lee, 55, 80, 84
Millikin, Sen. Eugene, 2
Mineral Leasing Act of 1920, 35, 38–39, 63, 66, 67–68
minimum wage, 188, 189, 217
Mining Law of 1872, 38, 39, 40, 42, 47, 48, 49, 66, 67, 68
Minnesota Democratic-Farmer Labor Party, 79
Mobil Oil Company, 32, 58, 61
Morris, Arthur, 103
Morris-plan bank, 103
mortgages, 95, 96, 106, 115
Moynihan, Daniel P., 206
Mutual Savings Banks of the Northeast, 98

National Association of Manufacturers, 81, 97

National Crime Commission, 218
National Recovery Administration, 95, 96
Neighborhood Youth Corps, 190, 213, 218
Neuberger, Sen. Maurine, 79, 99
Neuberger, Sen. Richard, 79
Norris, George, 26
Noyes, Alfred, 122

O'Connor, Frank, 75
office expenses (Senate and House, "quasi-political"), 85–89
offshore oil, 51–54
Oil Shale Advisory Board, 56
Oil Shale, Advisory Commission on, 42, 43, 55
Oil Shale Company, The (Tosco), 32, 36, 44, 69
old age assistance, 155, 157, 158, 159, 161, 162–165, 168–170, 172, 173–184, 193, 212
Operation Bronco, 37, 38
Orshansky, Mollie, 124, 125, 126, 127, 129, 130, 131, 132, 135, 138, 141, 145, 172, 177, 178, 189, 197
Other America, The, 123

Pan American Oil Company, 32
Pascal, Blaise, 216
patents, 60, 61
Patman, Rep. Wright, 21, 120
Paul, Randolph, 3

Pechman, Joseph, 12
Phillips, David Graham, 71
Phillips Oil Company, 32
poor, numbers of, 127–131, 135, 139, 145, 150, 151, 188, 190, 191, 193, 201
Poor People's Campaign, 124, 140
poor, statistical definitions of the, 124–127, 136, 137, 139, 141–142, 192, 201
poverty, causes of, 142–143, 189, 190, 201
poverty, war on, 190, 220, 221
Powell, Rep. Adam Clayton, 70
Poynter, Nelson, 55
Prescott, William H., 25
Proxmire, Sen. William, 14, 55, 86, 87, 99, 119, 121

Raglan, Lord, 14
residence requirements for public aid, 183–185
residue disposal (from shale deposits), 34–36, 37, 61–62
Rifle, Colorado, 31
Robertson, Sen. A. Willis, 97, 98, 99
Rockefeller, Gov. Nelson, 74, 75
Roosevelt, Franklin D., 144
Roosevelt, Theodore, 79
royalties, government (from oil), 52, 53, 56, 58–60, 62–65
Ruml plan, 5
Russell, Bertrand, 201

Russell Sage Foundation, 102, 103

Sanger, Margaret, 142
Schultz, Theodore, 147
Scott, Sir Walter, 27
Semer, Milton, 96
Shame of the Cities, The, 71
Sinclair Oil Company, 32
Snyder case (*Udall v. Snyder*), 66, 67
Social Rehabilitation Service, 172
Social Security Act of 1935, 154, 155, 156, 180
social security, 155–160, 177, 193
Sparkman, Sen. John, 132
Spong, Sen. William B., 99
Standard Oil of Indiana, 61
Standard Oil of Ohio (Sohio), 32
state, as employer of the poor, 194, 195, 213, 214, 217, 218
Steffens, Lincoln, 71
Stern, Philip, 5, 14, 15
stock options, 15–17
Sullivan, Rep. Leonore K., 100, 119, 120, 121
Surrey, Stanley, 3, 24
Switzer, Mary, 156

Taft, Sen. Robert, 73
tax, capital gains, 14–15, 16, 143
tax, dual income, 22–23

tax deductions for travel and entertainment, 20–21

tax exemptions for "charitable" contributions, 21

tax exemptions for homeowners, 21–22

tax, inheritance, 15, 17

tax, negative income, 194, 195, 202, 203, 206, 207, 208

tax, personal income, 4–9, 221

Teapot Dome, 46, 51

television and radio expenses, 85, 87

Tolstoy, Leo, 222

Townsend, Dr. F. E., 169, 184

Treason of the Senate, The, 71

truth-in-lending bill, 96–100, 110–121

Truth-in-Securities Act, 112

Ture, Dr. Norman, 3

Truman, Harry S., 1

Udall, Stewart L., 43, 46, 48, 50, 58, 60, 62, 65, 66

unemployed, chronically, 137–138, 157, 158, 181, 182, 186–192, 213, 217, 218, 219

unemployment compensation, 155–160, 180, 182, 186–187

unemployment, effects of, rate of, 136, 137, 147, 148

Union Oil Company of California, 32, 69

United Automobile Workers, 27

United Fund, 149

U.S. Chamber of Commerce, 97

U.S. Steel, 91

"Urban Coalition," 218

urban migration, 132–135, 148, 214, 218

Urban Problems, Commission on, 140

"vagabond's wage," 201

veterans' benefits, 160

Virginia-Colorado case (*Ickes v. Virginia-Colorado Development Company*), 43, 67, 68

Wages and Hours Act, 181

Walpole, Horace, 54

Walsh, Sen. Thomas, 51

Webster, Daniel, 91

Welfare, Advisory Council on Public, 208, 209

Wheeler, Sen. Burton K., 51

Williams, Sen. John, 12

Willkie, Wendell, 73

Winegar case, 69

Works Progress Administration (WPA), 156, 217

Zweifel, Bonnie E., 45

Zweifel, Maude H., 45

Zweifel, Merle L., 44–49, 66–67